Into PRINT

● SUSAN QUILLIAM ● IAN GROVE-STEPHENSEN

Published by BBC Books,
a division of BBC Enterprises Limited,
Woodlands, 80 Wood Lane, London W12 0TT
First published 1990
Reprinted 1992
© Transformation Management Ltd 1990

ISBN 0 563 21505 4

Set in 10 on 12pt Palatino
Printed in England by Clays Ltd, St Ives plc
Cover printed by Clays Ltd, St Ives plc, Norwich

Into PRINT

● SUSAN QUILLIAM ● IAN GROVE-STEPHENSEN

BBC BOOKS

CONTENTS

INTRODUCTION

There has never been a better time to get into print. We are in the middle of a revolution: the personal publishing revolution.

What has caused this revolution? It isn't only the improvement in computers. Of course, the technology has changed. Typesetting machines used to cost a fortune, and typesetting itself was an apprenticed trade. Now, with a difference in quality that is unnoticeable except to the trained eye, you can produce typeset text in your own living room via a computer that your children use for playing games.

But there is another, more subtle and infinitely more widespread change. Whether you use the technology or not, whether you are working with a high-powered computer or your old portable typewriter, you now know you can publish, that you are *able* to do it yourself.

This is the really revolutionary aspect to the publishing revolution. Not everyone has the technology yet – or wants it. But more and more people are able to wander into their local instant print shop with a rough sketch of a business card, and discuss it on an *equal* level with the printer behind the counter.

People are beginning to get involved. Getting into print is an attitude of involvement (even more than a technology that allows that involvement) and people are beginning to take it on board.

They are starting to realise that it is fun to take charge of one's own brochures, to make decisions about a letterhead, to typeset a church magazine. They are beginning to realise the total high to be got from seeing one's own leaflet roll off the photocopier, knowing that it has cost less time and less money, and has involved far more energy and creativity than if one had simply briefed a printer and then gone home.

It is not all plain sailing of course. There was a very good reason why, in the past, printing was done by skilled professionals. It consists of a series of highly skilled jobs: editing, design, typesetting, illustration control and production, not to mention the management of these tasks.

This book helps you develop not only the skills but also the strategies for personal publishing. It can give you the basic theoretical knowledge and a growing awareness of what works in practice. We hope it will also give you that sense of involvement, excitement and achievement that personal publishing can bring.

We hope this book will get *you* into print.

Past to present

Up to even 30 years ago, the publishing process had changed little over the past centuries. The writer wrote, the editor edited, the words were set, letter by letter. More recently, metal setting was replaced by photosetting and then photosetting was computerised.

Here, the words were typed into a computer and trained typesetters used complex computer codes to format the text. The result was a strip of photographic paper which could be pasted down on to card, along with any illustrations. A film of this master was taken and used to make the 'plate' used as the basis for printing. Finally, the whole was collated, bound and delivered. The cost was high, the time long. But there were few other choices.

Now, you have choice. Current personal computers, of the sort that most people can not only afford but learn to operate, can be used to produce text of near-typeset quality, and also to lay out text on the screen. Using a scanner, you can also include illustrations in the layout, so that the finished page is all on computer and doesn't need to be physically pasted up. You can then, if you choose, do the reproduction yourself, to eliminate even the trip to the printer.

This is the new technology. It saves time, labour, money; it gets high-quality results. You can opt into any part of it, combining the new methods of computer typesetting and page organisation with the older processes of printing and binding. You can call in the professionals at any point, or keep your publishing totally personal.

Traditional publishing process

New publishing process

What is the catch?

It sounds wonderful. The new approach to publishing gives you a flexible way of presenting anything you want in a high-quality way, quickly and cheaply.

So what's the problem? For there are problems. Before taking a detailed look at personal publishing, you may want to consider some of the pros and cons.

Pros

- It gives you more control over the process.
- If you are already having a document professionally published, you may well want to do it more cheaply...
- ... Or with a faster turn-round time.
- If you are not already having a document professionally produced, personal publishing is a way to create upmarket material where you couldn't before.
- Personal publishing can give you, or the team you work with, a real sense of involvement and achievement.
- It can be fun.

Cons

- Even using the new technology, personal publishing can look downmarket. For example, letters done on a laser printer have fuzzier outlines than typeset ones.
- Conversely, using the new technology can make material too upmarket, when readers want an approachable feel. A full-colour brochure to advertise your plumbing service makes you look over-priced.
- It can take more of your own time, and a lot more expertise. You may prefer to hand over the job to others.
- Personal publishing encourages people to dabble in skilled work such as design, and this can have appalling results.
- It can be costly: computers are not cheap.
- Many people don't like using computers.

Where personal publishing doesn't work is because you yourself haven't yet developed the strategies to do it properly. Notice we say strategies rather than skills. What makes personal publishers professional rather than amateur is whether they have generic management strategies, such as defining choices, planning, making decisions, working with others.

What this book offers

Knowledge
A framework of basic facts, and a reference appendix. In particular, we try to include comprehensive lists of the options available to you at each stage.

Skills
A basic grounding in a range of specific skills from writing the original text through to distributing your document, plus references to more in-depth sources for particular skills.

Strategies
Constant reference to strategies such as making choices, planning your work, maintaining quality control. We think these are the core of good personal publishing.

Models
A series of examples of publishing practice throughout the book, so you can begin to assess what works for you and what doesn't.

Profiles
A series of profiles of personal publishing practitioners and of helpful professionals, so you can understand and identify with them.

We use the following terms throughout this book. *Personal publishing*: any project you yourself are responsible for. *Desktop publishing* (or DTP): small-scale publishing specifically using the new technology. *Document*: any published work from a letterhead to a full length book. *Reader*: anyone who reads your document, from a friend to a nationwide corporate market.

2

FIRST IDEAS

First ideas are crucial. They inform and create your document. Ultimately, they dictate its success or failure.

The excitement that goes along with first ideas can tempt you to start production right away. In the long term, however, you will get a better document if, before turning ideas into decisions, you ask certain key questions to formulate your first ideas more accurately. This chapter asks those questions.

Who are your readers?

You first need to know who are the people you want to reach with your information. Readers for a business card will be different from readers for a sports magazine. Your possible market might be: customers, friends, those with a common interest, employees, the authorities, opinion formers.

How will you track them down? Formal market research is costly and usually unnecessary. List people you already know who will be your readers, then ask yourself who your readers might be if they knew about what you were doing. Then get to know them. Send out a questionnaire, ring them up.

Be nosey. Ask about your readers. What life-style do they live? Do they work, have children, read newspapers? Get a clear picture of who they are and what they do.

Also, be choosy. Decide who you want to reach and who not. If you aim to get new customers, you won't need to attract old ones.

Finally, be realistic. If you know your project won't work without a readership of 100, don't go ahead if you can only find 20.

What does the reader want?

Once you have found out who your readers are, it is good professional practice (and not just a party game) to spend some time 'identifying with' them and finding out what they really want.

Begin by imagining someone you know, maybe someone you've met while researching your market. Choose an actual person whose attitudes you are aware of and who would use your document. What sort of person are they? What is important to them? Why might they be interested in reading your document?

Now think more specifically about their attitudes to what you want to publish. If you were this person, what would you want to see, hear and feel when you were handed this document? Ask detailed questions. Would it be important that it was in colour? Would it need to be on heavy paper? Would you want it to have several pages, be easily storable, be long-lasting? Imagine making very specific judgements about a document, and be clear on what your potential user would like or dislike.

What do you want?

What do you as a publisher want? Depending on exactly what your document is, you may have a variety of aims. Do you need to boost sales, invite people to your wedding, spread information, contact the community, create a credible image, entertain and amuse? Take the time to get really clear on your outcomes.

How do you want your readers to feel? Warm and friendly as they open your community newsletter? Impressed and convinced as they handle your business card?

Are you perhaps dealing with already existing negative feelings that you want to combat, as when you are producing a study guide or a no-smoking leaflet?

What action do you want your readers to take? Do you want them to get more involved in the community? Buy your plumbing service? Go on the march? And, in order to take this action, do the readers need more than just feelings – do they need information, suggestions, direction?

What type of document?

Next think about the context in which your document will be used.

Where? On a wall or during a personal meeting? In a busy or quiet environment? Against a background of or alongside other things that will compete? On the move or standing still? A poster needs a very different presentation from that of a business card.

When? Day, afternoon, evening, night? Before or after another event? How regularly; is this a one-off wedding menu or a weekly newsletter? How long will this product be used for? Is it meant to last for a day, as in the case of an exhibition leaflet; for years, as with a book? How durable and storable must it be?

What reading pattern will the document demand? Browsing, as with a magazine? Reading for long periods, as people do with books? Glancing and looking away, as with a poster? Scanning to find information, as with a timetable or reference work?

The questions listed on these two pages will help you to decide what kind of document you need.

RHM GROCERY

THE 1988 RHM CONFERENCE CHALLENGE

NAME OF TEAM: _____

THE CHURCH OF THE HOLY CROSS

Easter is upon us - it is a time when Christians celebrate the death and resurrection of Jesus, and the time when all of us celebrate the return of Spring. It is a time to enjoy the new life which is all about us. So from Easter onwards our evening services will be at 7pm, this will give us the opportunity to use the longer hours of daylight. Why not come along and join us? Please note that there is no evening service on the second or fourth Sundays of the month.

Have a Joyful Easter,
Your Friend and Minister,
Dorothy Spence.

Services this month
April
2nd 10.45am Service with
        Mr. Don Scrimshaw
    7.00pm Service with
        Miss Marion Wright
9th 10.45am Holy Communion
16th 10.45am Service with
        Infant Dedication
        & Infant Baptism
    7.00pm Evening of Praise
23rd 10.45am Holy Communion
30th 10.45am Service with
        Infant Baptisms
    7.00pm Service with
        Mr. Greg Simmons

May
7th 9.30am Holy Communion
    10.45am Family Service
    7.00pm Service with
        Mr. Bill Thomas

CHURCH NEWS

WANTED URGENTLY
HOLM BASE MANAGEMENT COMMITTEE urgently require a voluntary secretary to attend a monthly meeting for about two hours to take the minutes, type them up and circulate them to the members. In addition 3-4 letters will need to be sent. A typewriter is available. The work of the community is active and lively and the secretary will find it both interesting and rewarding. If you are interested, please phone Jeff Fawcett on MK 692692 extension 2423.

page 6

COURSE 1
MACINTOSH FOR BEGINNERS - A One Day Course

This is the perfect introductory course for users coming to the Apple Macintosh for the first time. No prior experience is assumed and our trainers will slowly and carefully explain all basic Macintosh operations, from switch on to document creation and printing.

We never train in groups larger than three people so individual attention is assured. The elements of this course include basic machine operation, mouse and screen management techniques, file creation and handling, the file structure of the Macintosh, basic computing tasks including document creation, editing (copy, paste, cut and print) and information safety procedures. Also included are techniques of virus detection and prevention.

Cost per day £130 per person (in a group of 3 or less)

COURSE 2
INTRODUCTION TO DESKTOP PUBLISHING 1 - A One Day Course

This foundation course in desktop publishing provides all of the basic skills necessary to start producing simple pages in the popular page make-up programs. This course assumes a basic familiarity with the Macintosh.

The programs introduced during this day include word-processing packages, Aldus PageMaker 3.0, Quark Xpress 2.1, Ready Set Go 4.5 and a tour of various graphics programs including Mac Paint, MacDraw II, Aldus Freehand and Adobe Illustrator.

At the end of this one day course attendees will have a broad overview of the capabilities and component programs of professional DTP.

Cost per day £130 per person (in a group of 3 or less)

COURSE 3
INTRODUCTION TO DESKTOP

We often su...
days. Part...
tools of DT...
Adobe Ill...
and pag...
covered...

At the...
prod...
familiar w...

Cost per day £130 p...

En-igma ™
TYPESETTING · DESIGN &

What works and what doesn't

On the page opposite, we have presented some samples of personally published documents. Ask yourself these questions about each of them.

Would *your* readers like it? Would it create the impression, the feelings, the responses you want? Would it be effective in the place you want to use your product, at the time you will be using it, for the relevant reading pattern?

It is obvious that some of the samples on the opposite page will be totally useless for your purposes. It's also obvious that, without reading the rest of this book, it will be impossible for you to make detailed decisions. However, asking questions such as the ones we suggest will begin to give you an essential strategy for desktop publishing – that of judging if a document and the way it has been produced is suitable for your purposes and likely to appeal to your reader.

We suggest that you develop this strategy over a period of at least a week before making any firm decisions.

- Collect as many samples as you can of the kind of product you are thinking of publishing. Then spend time not only looking at the samples but also handling them. Show them to other people and get their reactions. Which work, and which don't?
- Start looking out for differences in these areas: kind of document; size of document; size of pages; use of illustration, colour, typestyle.
- Talk to someone who would use your product. Show them your samples. Ask

them to tell you in detail what impresses them or puts them off. Tape record the conversation for better recall.
- If you have a project team, ask what their views are. They will add to your impression of what the user wants, and will also help you firm up your ideas.
- Talk to experts – designers, printers, typesetters – about what their experience of your user is. At this stage, don't listen too much to what they say about how to make your product. Listen first for what they suggest your product should be.
- Look at what the most successful people in your field are doing. Is this the impression you want to make? How could you alter the doument to make it more suitable for your users?
- What are the least successful people in your field doing? What mistakes are they making that you can avoid?
- If your document is a big-budget one, hire in professional help. A market research company can tell you what your user wants by going out and asking.
- Keep developing your awareness: each time you handle a book, magazine, letterhead, ask if it really has the effect it is aiming at. If so, how? If not, why not?

Can you do it?

Having developed your ability to decide what works and what doesn't, you will almost certainly have firmed up your conception of what your product should be. You will have rough ideas on all the following.

- Format (type of document).
- Size (number and size of pages).
- Print run (how many you will print).
- Use of illustrations (style, colour, etc).
- Cost (how much you wish to spend).
- Schedule (how long you wish to take).

Don't expect to have a fully formed specification at this stage. Detailed decisions will come later, as you gain a clearer idea of what is possible. However, check now whether your broad-based plans are viable.

- Budget: get a rough estimate by deciding what you want in general terms, then checking prices with the subcontractors most likely to have substantial costs. Can you afford to go ahead?
- Time: make a rough estimate of the time factor by finding out from all the people involved how long they will take. Do you need to publish by a particular deadline? Is the project possible in the time you have?
- Skills: as we point out later in the book, it may be better to subcontract skilled work to get a more effective product. Work out how much of the work you can do yourself, cross-reference that to budget and time. Is the project still viable?
- Other resources: will you need equipment, contacts, information? If you can get them, how much time, money and energy will you expend to do so?

	What you need	What you have	How to make it work
Budget			
Time			
Skills			
Other resources			

Our varying projects demand different letterheads, which could have meant an expensive series of different papers and logos. Our solution was to have a single logo printed in different colours on white paper. The different text elements – our name(s), address, project phone number – are printed from the computer along with each letter they head up.

Making it work

So can you do it? It could be, having examined your broad-based plans, that they just don't seem viable. A key strategy throughout any personal publishing project is matching your aims with your resources, and being able to come up with solutions if they don't match.

If you hit problems, now or throughout your project, begin by asking two questions.

- How can you change your ideas?
- How can you gather more resources?

Then, brainstorm solutions. Below is a list of some solutions that people we talked to adopted to solve their problems.

- Problem: not enough money.
  Solutions: get sponsorship; sell advertising space; cut down number of pages; change to a cheaper distributor; borrow hardware.
- Problem: not enough time.
  Solutions: advertise for help in parish magazine; cancel one edition of the newsletter; publish series of books separately rather than all at once.
- Problem: not enough skills.
  Solutions: pool skills with specialists in other fields; take evening class in community printing; make friends with local typesetter; buy in marketing distribution services.
- Problem: not enough other resources.
  Solutions: use community resource centre equipment; join computer user clubs and get support; go to exhibitions and tout for business and contacts.

Sandra Corbin

Main Event is a new, free glossy magazine for active Londoners. Unlike other freebies in the capital, however, it was started as a personal publishing project by one woman with no business experience and little money.

Sandra Corbin caught the publishing bug when, at 15, she won a poetry competition and saw her work in print. She joined the London office of the *Gleaner*, Jamaica's leading newspaper, as a trainee journalist. Then, freelancing while taking a business studies course, she 'saw the mistakes others were making, and thought I could do it better'.

With her Enterprise Allowance boosted by £1000 each from the Prince's Trust and her area Enterprise Agency, she bought two computers and a laser printer. She took outside jobs and did 'shiftwork, anything to pay the bills'. She wrote to art colleges saying she had an exciting project, not much money, and needed a graphic designer. She found Suren Gunputh, whose bold style is now indelibly stamped on the magazine. It was also necessary to find help from writers and assistants who believed in the concept of *Main Event*.

Sandra is clear about her market: 'it's the type of person I would mix with socially – 18-30 years old, and ambitious'. Copy that has been submitted stands the best chance of being used if it is 'something that *is* a main event'. It can fail at the last minute, however. 'If someone says, "I'm bored typing this in", I think, "in that case, who'll read it?"'.

Being free, the magazine relies on advertising for revenue, and advertisers need to see it is being read before supporting it. At first, it was given away outside Tube stations. Now, Sandra is more selective: 'we send it to libraries, business centres, hairdressers – anywhere it will be seen by lots of people'.

The magazine is still in its early stages, but Sandra is sure she will make it. She's not the only one. On a wall of the spare room that is *Main Event*'s corporate headquarters hangs her runner's up certificate for the 'Woman of Tomorrow' Award.

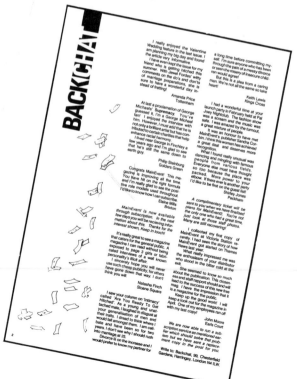

Quality control

Getting things right at the start is one problem. Keeping them right throughout the production process – and on into years of reprints – is another.

Throughout this book, we assume that you yourself will be aiming for high quality. Far more challenging is the ability to control the quality of other people you work with or subcontractors, such as typesetters or artists.

Here are some generic points that apply throughout the process.

- Check quality at every stage. Know what to look for, and look regularly.
- Get a clear idea of the standards you can expect from yourself and other people, and what it is unreasonable or impossible to expect.
- When finding people to work with, always check their price, their availability, their track record.
- When negotiating price, check whether it includes expenses, whether it is a fixed fee or charged by time (hourly rates soon mount up) and what happens if you ask for changes.
- Where you can, make contracts about your expectations. These can be verbal or written and should include the work to be done, the price and the time to be taken.
- When briefing, always explain who your reader is and what the aims of your document are; this will help other people to work for you more effectively.
- Where possible, check work at an early stage, to catch early misunderstandings.
- Always allow more time for each job than you have admitted to other people.
- When you see something wrong in the work done, ask for changes immediately.
- When the price is higher than promised, query it immediately and *before* paying.
- When deadlines are due, ring a few days beforehand to ask courteously if the work will be there on time. If the answer is no, negotiate for an arrangement that will allow you to cut time elsewhere.
- Get feedback throughout the production process – from the people you work with and from key users.

As long as your document is in preparation, keep asking three basic questions. What do my readers want the document to do? What do I want the document to do? Is it doing both of these? If not, something needs to change.

FIRST DECISIONS

First decisions about your document will alter as your situation changes, or as crises occur, but they do need to be made before you can start work.

Here, we firstly provide you with a flow chart overview of what decisions need to be made. Secondly, the chapter includes three fill-in charts to guide you through the processes of scheduling, production and cost.

There is, of course, a 'Catch 22'. The material in this chapter all relates to topics that are covered in detail during the course of the book. You may therefore not be able to use the flow charts and fill-in charts fully until you have worked your way through the following chapters. This problem is, unfortunately, in the nature of linear presentation. Roll on the truly interactive book!

What happens when?

The order in which events happen varies enormously from publisher to publisher and project to project. We have tried to draw up a flow chart showing a typical process, but you will have your own amendments to make.

On page 20 is a scheduling chart. As each document has its own schedule, you may want to change this too to fit your timing. If this is your first project, allow more time than you think you will need!

With the new technology, some of the more costly processes can now be left until later in the production schedule. Equally, you can finalise design specifications at an earlier stage. Use this, by briefing your staff as fully as you can as early as you can. Conversely, beware the fact that, while traditional publishing demands up-front decisions and no changes of mind, personal publishing allows alterations. It can be a 'licence for sloppiness' as one publisher calls it, and certainly you need to build into your schedule time for final panics and about-turns.

If you do run over schedule, call your subcontractors (particularly your printer if you are using one) as soon as you know there is a problem, otherwise you may find they cannot fit you in at a later time.

The production process

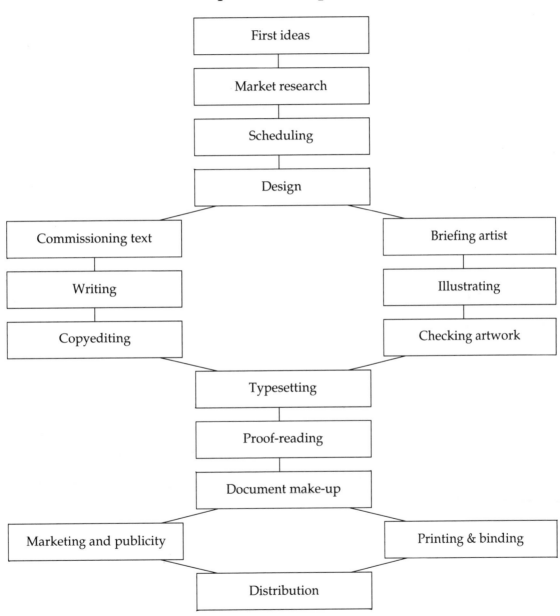

Scheduling chart

Job

Time taken
Date begun
Date completed

Decision on first ideas
Document design
Production design
Pricing and budgeting of subcontracted work
Writing of text
Illustrations
Editing
Typesetting
Checking of illustrations
Proofing
Printing
Job complete
Marketing and publicity

Document specification chart

This chart lists all the main decisions that you will need to make when designing your document.

N.B. *denotes a specification element that only applies in certain cases, e.g. if you are sub-contracting the work.

Document name

Document design (Chapter 4)
Designer*
Format of document
Number of pages
Paper size
Paper shape
Page depth
Margins
Grid — column sizes,
   gutter sizes etc

Length of print run

Writer(s) (Chapter 5)

Illustrations (Chapter 6)
Illustrator*
Source*
Number of illustrations
Sizes
Placing
Colour
Enlargement or
 reduction needed
Screening needed

Editing (Chapter 5)
Commissioning editor*
Copy editor*
Proof-reader*
Technology (Chapter 8)
Typesetter*
Software to be used*

Design for title and other special pages (Chapter 7)
Half-title
Title
Imprint or
   bibliographical page
Contents
Illustration list
Introduction
Footnotes
Index
Annotation

Design of text pages (Chapter 7)

specification for main text
font
point size
leading
measure
ranging
justification
caps
ital/bold/distorted text
para division, indent
text indent
hyphenation on or off

specification main head
font
point size
leading
measure
range
centre
caps
ital/bold/distorted text

specification subhead 1
font
point size
leading
measure
range
centre
caps
ital/bold/distorted text

specification subhead 2
font
point size
leading
measure
range
centre
caps
ital/bold/distorted text

specification subhead 3
font
point size
leading
measure
range
centre
caps
ital/bold/distorted text

specification illustration captions
font
point size
leading
measure
range
centre
positioning
caps
ital/bold/distorted text
para division, indent

Running titles
Font
Headers
Footers
Pagination

Special design features
Rules
Boxes
Tint panels
Arrows
Box asterisks
Initial letter capping

Cover
Cover illustrator*

Preproduction (Chapter 9)
Paste-up artist*
Paste-up details –
   how mounted
Colour separations
   required
Enlargement, reduction,
   cropping
Screening required

Production (Chapter 10)
Paper supplier*
Printer*
Binder*
Special finisher*

Paper spec for text:
   size, type, weight, colour
Paper spec for cover:
   size, type, weight, colour
Other paper spec: size,
   type, weight, colour
End papers: size, type,
   weight, colour
Boards: size, type,
   weight, colour
Number of colours
Envelopes required*
Special finishes required
Collating required
Binding required
Special presentation
   covers required
Reproduction to be
   done by (on) machine

Post-production (Chapter 11-12)
Distribution*
Marketing*

Any other personnel involved:
Secretary
Financial advisor
Envelope stuffers

Price at which to be sold

Budgeting chart

The chart gives a very rough guide to budgeting for a book. A magazine would involve continuing expenses and would need a different type of budget. We suggest that as initial quotes for jobs may vary, and prices may change, you expect to copy and fill in this form a number of times, from the initial estimate through to a final budget. Of course, if you intend to publish commercially, you should take professional financial advice.

Money in:	
Sales	
(number of copies printed x price less any discount)	£
Other sources: grants, sponsorship, bank loan, personal funding	£
Money out:	
Market research	£
Document design	£
Research	£
Clerical support	£
Writing	£
Illustrations	£
Photography	£
Computer graphics	£

Copyediting	£
Proof-reading	£
Typesetting	£
Paste-up and preproduction preparation, enlargement, reduction, cropping etc	£
Paper (if separate from printing) for text/for covers	£
Printing, photocopying	£
Special finishes	£
Binding	£
Marketing	£
Distribution	£
General expenses:	
accommodation, heating, lighting	£
stationery	£
postage and packing	£
travel	£
artwork materials	£
telephone	£
labour costs for packing	£
Initial quote	£
Final quote	£
Total	£
Balance	£

CHAPTER 4

DOCUMENT DESIGN

By document design, we mean the visual appearance of the document: its size, format, layout, style.

When deciding these, however, you have to consider other elements. The process is interactive and you will create your document design whilst deciding these things: how will the document be read? (Chapter 2); what text and how much text? (Chapter 5); which illustrations and how many? (Chapter 6); which typestyle? (Chapter 7); which production methods? (Chapter 10)

Overall format

Start, as we suggested in Chapter 2, by finding examples of the type of document you want to produce, and looking at what needs to go in it. Identify the elements in detail. The elements for a compliments slip, for example, might be: name; address; phone and fax number; the 'with compliments'. Those for a book might be: title page; dedication; copyright details; acknowledgements; contents; illustration list (these together are called prelims); text; captions; appendices; index.

What implications do these elements have for the overall format of your document? Should it be a small card or a large book, a single page or a series of leaflets? What order

should these elements fall in? Don't get hooked by convention; a wedding invitation could be in the form of a small leaflet if you want it to be.

Number of pages

You will obviously need enough space for the text and illustrations you want to include – though you will need to edit if there is a slight mismatch. But there are other issues to consider. What binding do you want to use? If you are having a stapled binding, you need a document with pages in units of four to enable folding in sections. (Not as tricky as it sounds – it is often easy to add three or cut one.) If you are reproducing single sheets, then the number is irrelevant – although, for any document, stop to consider if you are printing on one or both sides of the page.

Restaurant menu

The Hong Kong Chinese Restaurant in Barking, Essex, has been open for some years, an ordinary Chinese restaurant serving ordinary food.

Recently, owner-manager Mr Li decided to revamp. As he explained, 'we wanted to bring up the standard of the restaurant. Before, we served Chop Suey and things like that. Now we want to move upmarket and get a different type of customer.' As well as completely redecorating, Mr Li decided to offer more sophisticated food. This meant producing a more sophisticated menu.

Like most small businessmen, Mr Li was a regular customer at his local instant print shop, in this case Prontaprint. There, graphic artist Gill Bush already had a wealth of experience of what would and what would not work with restaurant menus.

She explained that 'a menu must be simple, and easily recognisable for what it is'. She chose the typeface Benguiat because it is 'legible, clean and unfussy, but not boring. You can read it even in subdued lighting even when you have been drinking. That's crucial in a restaurant!' Matched with the simple lotus design that she created to carry through all his stationery, Benguiat imparts an oriental feel to the document without being clichéd.

Gill chose beige for the heavy menu paper and teamed this not with a predictable black, but with burgundy ink, giving a subtle and elegant feel to the whole design.

All the stationery was prepared on Prontaprint's DTP system. As well as speeding turn-around, this will also make it much easier to update menus from time to time. This creates repeat business for the shop, and maintains the restaurant's efficient image.

Having given Gill a totally free hand to design the menu, Mr Li is happy with the result. 'We get a different type of customer, people who are much more relaxing to serve.' So the menus, as part of a package of changes to the restaurant, have not only improved business; they have improved the quality of life of the people who work there, too.

Special Set Dinners
Prix Fix Menu

A

For 2 - £11.00 per person

Imperial Combination of Three Delicacies
Chicken & Sweet Corn Soup

Sweet & Sour Pork
Beef with Spring Onion
Chicken with Green Pepper & Black Bean Sauce
Egg Fried Rice

Choice of Sweet

B

For 2 - £12.00 per person

Spare Ribs with Sauce
Prawn Crackers

Crispy Aromatic Duck

Deep Fried Shredded Beef with Chilli
Fried Chicken with Lemon Sauce
Red Hot Pork 'Szechuan Style'
Egg Fried Rice

Choice of Sweet

C

For 3 - £13.50 per person

Imperial Combination of Three Delicacies

Crispy Aromatic Duck

Sliced Beef with Chilli

Page size and shape

What page size is right for your document? Letter stationery is usually A4, the 'normal page size', compliments slips are one-third A4. Book sizes vary, while a good size for newsletters is A5 (half an A4). For more about page sizes see page 178.

What page shape is relevant? Landscape format has page width greater than depth, and is useful for showing long illustrations, but if used for a book is awkward to hold and store. Portrait format is the normal book shape. Square is suitable for documents where you have a variety of illustration shapes.

Page templates

How will the text and illustrations fit on the page? Obviously each page of your document will be different, but making all your text and illustrations conform to the same general layout will give your document a cohesive feel. A page template is a basic page layout which runs through the whole document and into which you fit the content. Factors to be considered in designing templates are these.

Margins

How wide will your margins be? It is better to have your foot margin greater than your head margin, or your text will seem as if it were falling off the page. Look particularly at how pairs of pages that are going to face each other (a spread) look together, remembering that they need to be mirror images of each other, with the margins set accordingly. Remember to allow extra left-hand margin space of about 5.0-7.5 mm if you are wiro or ring binding.

Columns

Will you arrange your text on the page in one, two, three, four (or even five) columns? For an A4 page, one column is often too broad to read easily; two columns is more legible. An A5 page can usually cope with one column. Newspapers use several columns, which allow easy browsing through small chunks of text. Columns don't all have to be the same size on a page, though they usually are. You can also flow text or illustrations across a column to create interest.

The space between columns is called a gutter, and you will obviously work out how wide your gutters are to be in conjunction with how wide your margins and columns are. If you want to divide columns more obviously, then use rules (lines) between them.

Horizontal divisions

These are a horizontal version of columns, dividing your page into boxes. They encourage you to divide text or include illustrations at regular points, and so help you give each page a more cohesive feel. They can also be emphasised with rules.

Headers and footers

These are sections of text that appear regularly on every page. They can be the name of the document, chapter or section, or the page numbering, and they normally go on the top or bottom outer edge of the page, or centred on the page area.

Adobe

Adobe Systems Incorporated

1585 Charleston Road • P.O. Box 7900 • Mountain View, CA 94039-7900 •

The NeXT™ Computer System

One New England Executive Park • Burlington, MA 01803

Benefits of the Display PostScript System

While PostScript® printers, typesetters and film recorders have set new standards for hard copy, display technology has lagged behind. Because displays and printers used different imaging models – the method for describing the appearance of text, graphics and scanned images – what you saw on screen was not quite what you got in printed output. Times have changed.

▲ *A unified imaging model for both display and printer ensures true WYSIWYG.*

Unified Imaging Model

The NeXT Computer uses the Display PostScript® system, a high-performance implementation of the PostScript

Software applications will automatically on all displays supported by NeXT. T encourages innovations in display te while maintaining application com

More Powerful Application Softw

Applications that use the Display P system exhibit more powerful feat finally, software developers can ea power of the PostScript language Display PostScript environments, software packages are limited by and graphics operations support computer. Also, valuable time is device drivers for incompatible printers instead of programmin functionality for end users.

With the Display PostScript s limitations are removed, and clearly visible on screen: font Type Library at any size and control over graphics includ and realistic halftone image be rotated and scaled.

The Adobe Type Library

The Display PostScript

What?

What do we do?

Plain English is
specialising in

at is, we wr
ruction bo

ther you
00-pag
o the
ds:

company | Here are just a few examples of the work
we have performed for our clients to

Signs Illuminaire

Unit 11, Riverside Industrial Estate,
27 Thames Road, Barking, Essex.
Telephone 01-594 7516

AVON POETRY FESTIVAL
PRESENTS

Anne Stevenson
new poetry

ANNE STEVENSON WAS BORN
IN ENGLAND OF
AMERICAN PARENTS IN 1933.
HER POETRY COLLECTIONS
INCLUDE *ENOUGH OF GREEN*
(1977), *MINUTE BY GLASS
MINUTE* (1982), AND *THE
FICTION MAKERS* (1985) SHE
IS ALSO THE AUTHOR OF THE
DEFINITIVE MAJOR
BIOGRAPHY OF SYLVIA
PLATH *BITTER FAME* TO BE
PUBLISHED IN THIS COUNTRY
IN THE AUTUMN.

ANNE STEVENSON'S RICHNESS
AND INVENTION MARK HER AS
ONE OF THE FEW
OUTSTANDING POETS NOW
WRITING IN ENGLISH ABLE
TO BALANCE EXTREMES OF
JOY AND SORROW WITHIN THE
TIGHT DISCIPLINE OF
SUBTLE RHYTHM AND PIN-
SHARP VISUAL VOCABULARY.

'England? You live in England?
   cried my New York taxi driver,
      'Why don't you live someplace

you can make a few bucks?'
   I want bucks.
      I want you more than bucks,

O England of the old books
   that never was until it
      finds itself in us.

TICKETS:
£2.00 / £1.25 concs.
AVAILABLE FROM CHAPTER &
VERSE BOOKSHOP.

APF

**Thursday May 25th 7.30pm
Chapter & Verse Park St, Bristol**

These samples all use different layout templates, and show variations in margins, text columns, headers and footers, and horizontal divisions.

Page design

Once you have decided on your basic document template, you then create the particular design for each page – what text and which illustrations go on which page, and where they go for greatest effect.

Types of reading material

In the western world, the pattern of reading is from top to bottom, left to right. Fiction and factual books normally follow this format. However, newspapers, magazines and brochures often divide the material so that the reader can skim around the page. Particular items of interest or explanation can also be 'pulled out' in boxes, surrounded by rules or filled with tint.

In advertisements, material is often divided into chunks, to be read in random order; return forms are sometimes placed at the bottom so readers come to them after being convinced by everything else on the page!

Symmetry or asymmetry

You need not have page designs (or templates) that are symmetrical, particularly for 'bitty' documents such as magazines or mail-outs. It is usually more lively if the elements within each grid are arranged irregularly. Whichever format you opt for, symmetrical or asymmetrical, don't mix the two layouts in one document.

White space

White space is any space not printed on. How much will you have on each page? Don't feel you have to fill up all the page area; use empty space in the same way as you would illustrations, to create interest.

Preparing a rough design

One of the best ways of developing your ideas about document design is to do roughs to see how each of your ideas might look.

At first, simply play with ideas, drawing small sketches. Do several scaled-down versions, with different column layouts and big and small typefaces (see Chapter 7).

When you have found a layout that you think might suit, draw it full size. Get correct-sized paper – preferably paper samples of the kind you think you might use for the finished document. Don't bother doing any more than boxes for illustrations and squiggly lines for text. If you are planning colour, use felt-tipped pen for effect. You will probably try several versions of a layout before you decide on a template that will really suit.

Once you have an accurate idea of the content of your document, do roughs for each page. For this book, we did 'thumbnails', scaled-down roughs on computer, eight per A4 sheet, with different shadings to indicate text and illustrations. This allowed us to keep track of each page and how much space each item would take.

If you are working on computer, this is the time to set up a full-size version of your template, into which you can type or flow your text.

If you are binding your document by stitching, you may need to present your pages to the printer in a particular arrangement called an imposition(see further details and the drawing on page 166). It is a good idea to plan your imposition at this stage so that you can check with the printer that it will work.

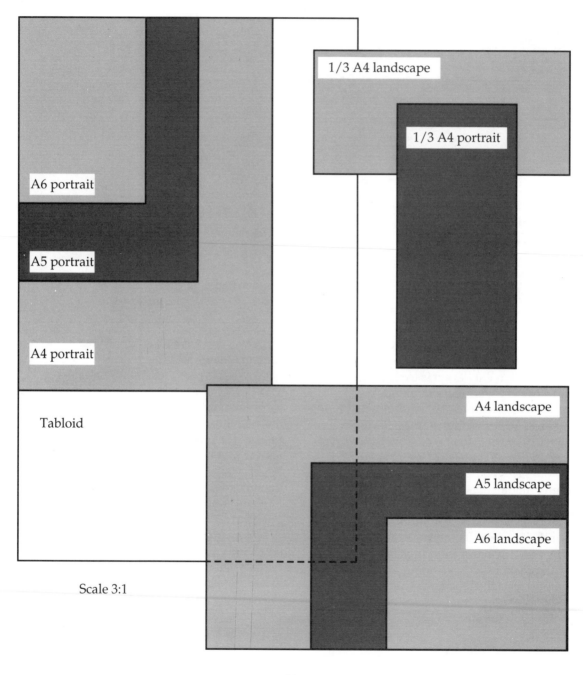

A6 portrait

A5 portrait

A4 portrait

Tabloid

Scale 3:1

1/3 A4 landscape

1/3 A4 portrait

A4 landscape

A5 landscape

A6 landscape

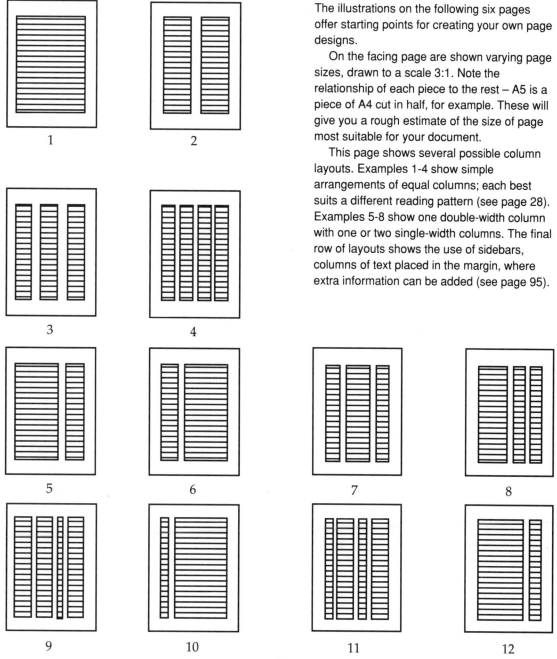

The illustrations on the following six pages offer starting points for creating your own page designs.

On the facing page are shown varying page sizes, drawn to a scale 3:1. Note the relationship of each piece to the rest – A5 is a piece of A4 cut in half, for example. These will give you a rough estimate of the size of page most suitable for your document.

This page shows several possible column layouts. Examples 1-4 show simple arrangements of equal columns; each best suits a different reading pattern (see page 28). Examples 5-8 show one double-width column with one or two single-width columns. The final row of layouts shows the use of sidebars, columns of text placed in the margin, where extra information can be added (see page 95).

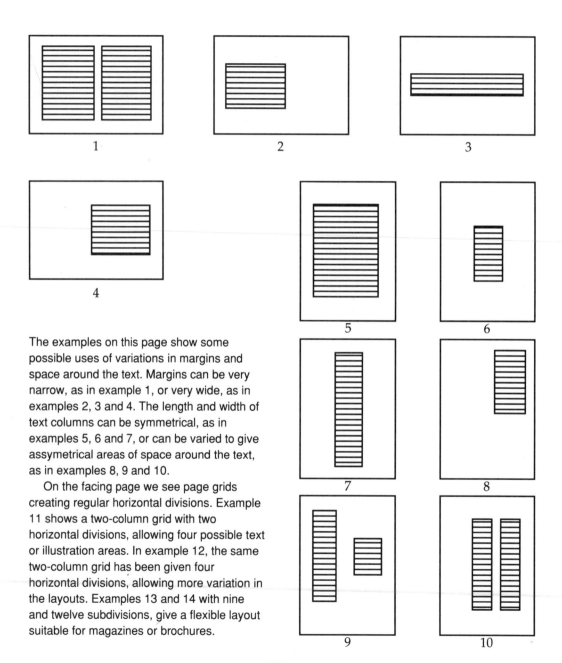

The examples on this page show some possible uses of variations in margins and space around the text. Margins can be very narrow, as in example 1, or very wide, as in examples 2, 3 and 4. The length and width of text columns can be symmetrical, as in examples 5, 6 and 7, or can be varied to give assymetrical areas of space around the text, as in examples 8, 9 and 10.

On the facing page we see page grids creating regular horizontal divisions. Example 11 shows a two-column grid with two horizontal divisions, allowing four possible text or illustration areas. In example 12, the same two-column grid has been given four horizontal divisions, allowing more variation in the layouts. Examples 13 and 14 with nine and twelve subdivisions, give a flexible layout suitable for magazines or brochures.

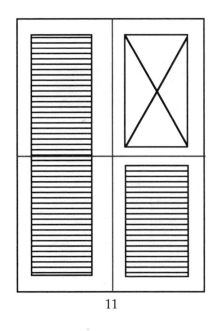

11

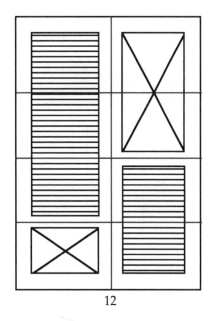

12

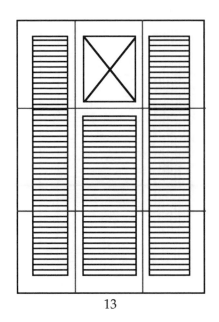

13

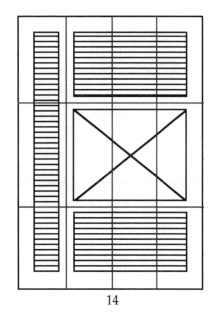

14

1

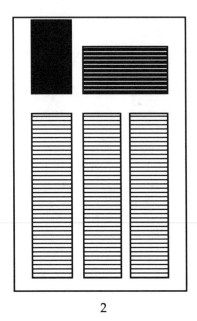

2

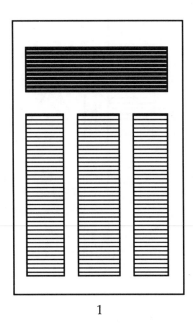

3

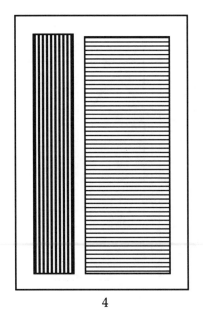

4

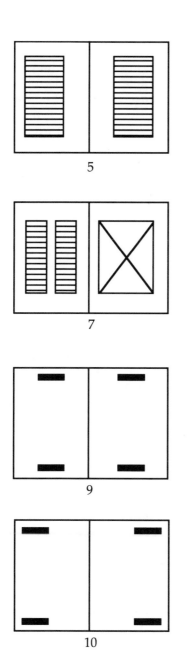

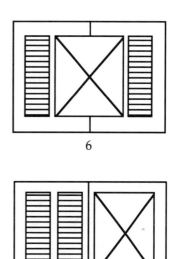

5

6

7

8

9

10

The facing page shows positions for mastheads – headlines and related information. Examples 1, 2 and 3 use a three-column layout with varying mastheads combining with varying lengths of column. In example 4, the masthead runs vertically alongside a double-width column of text. This page shows a selection of double-page spreads which highlight the fact that when planning a document, you need to consider how each page looks in relation to the one opposite. Examples 5-8 use a variety of layouts, including one in which an illustration crosses the spread, with accompanying production problems! Note how varying the position of text and illustrations within the spread gives a different feel to each one. Finally, examples 9 and 10 show the most usual positions for headers and footers.

Working with designers

You may choose not to attempt the document design yourself, but ask a designer to do it. The designer's job is to plan the overall look of a document as opposed to doing individual illustrations, which is an artist's work.

If you do, you may also be asking the designer to make decisions not only about a single document, but also about all the documents you will do from now on. If you get a house design for your football club programmes, then you will have a style for the next 10 seasons, not just the next match. So you need to get the designer – and the design – absolutely right.

Finding a designer

You will not find designers easy to track down; you need to be 'part of the system', as one designer put it, to know the good ones. Ask your printer or artist for recommendations. If you have neither of these, buy *Creative Handbook*, a magazine that includes listings, and look for those describing themselves as 'graphic' designers. Ring to check whether a designer will be willing to handle your project, checking rates before making an appointment – many who are used to the corporate market will be charging accordingly!

We found a wonderful source of fresh talent by contacting the careers office of our local art college and having them place a permanent ad in their newsletter. You may need to sift through poor quality to find the real talent, but when you find it he or she will be hugely enthusiastic and grateful. However, don't underpay artists just because they are newly qualified or still learning.

Choosing a designer

When meeting, begin by assessing just how far the designer is in sympathy with you and what you are doing. Look at his (or her) portfolio and decide whether you want to use him. If you do, discuss terms. Typically, you then brief the designer on just what your needs are, and he comes back with roughs from which you choose. If you like nothing of what he does, you need not proceed at this stage, although you will probably pay a rejection fee.

Briefing a designer

Take the time to explain just what your message is and how you want to affect your market. The designer ought to be able to tell you exactly how to do this; you ought to be able to enthuse him with your aims.

Then, give him as much background information as possible. What sort of text, and how much? What kind of illustrations and how many? Don't attempt to preempt things by telling the designer what you think he should do, but remember that the designer is trained to tease out what your needs are, and, if he doesn't come up with a design that works, he isn't doing his job.

Quality control

Designers charge by the hour or by the job. Check whether this includes expenses and materials, and if not how much these are likely to cost. Ask to see roughs of everything, to allow you to check quality and scheduling. If you don't like a design, say so at as early a stage as possible, and keep going until you get something that really works for you.

Michael Lopategui

Michael Lopategui is an independent graphic designer who runs his company, Design Effect, from a small modern studio in Fulham. His work includes creating leaflets, brochures, magazine adverts and promotional designs. Two years ago, we turned to him to create a striking image for our company and he came up with the logo on page 15, which we still use on all our stationery.

When we interviewed Michael, he was putting the finishing touches to a brochure for the Irish Tourist Board. The brochure is intended to promote Ireland as a venue for conferences and 'incentive travel' (holidays as prizes to you and me). Michael explained, 'It's important to understand your market'. Michael's first concern was to find an image that would evoke a feeling of Ireland. 'You learn to ask yourself "does this image mean shampoo or does it mean weedkiller?"' In this case, he settled on emotive landscape photography matched with subtle typography as the visual theme ('device' in designer jargon) for the brochure.

It is this ability to create an evocative image that Michael sees as the designer's main job. 'Your designer's contribution is to inform you what patterns, colours and styles have what meaning in today's market and to match these to your specific brief.' His favourite clients are those who tell him the effect they want him to create, but leave him the freedom to use his skill to achieve it. 'Some clients will do nothing more than ask me to go away and draw what they have described. Others will grossly overgeneralise and ask for an ad "as upmarket as Harrods, as fashionable as Habitat but with the mass appeal of MFI".'

Once the image is fixed in his mind, Michael will usually prepare a number of 'visuals', several variations on themes mocked up on presentation board, to give a general idea of design solutions. His job when presenting these is to 'sell the style'. Once Michael has the client's approval, he then goes on to the more technical stages of producing the finished item.

CHAPTER 5

FINDING THE WORDS

What is your message?

Identifying the message your document carries is the starting point for finding the words (and the pictures – see Chapter 6).

Think back to the earlier section of this book in which we suggested that you imagine yourself as the reader of your document. What message is this reader going to respond to? What message are you trying to give?

Almost certainly there will be an obvious message, the one that the words explicitly state, and an implicit message, the one that is suggested. The explicit message of a leaflet exhorting you to 'Buy Brown's Bread' is a clear direction. The implicit message in the words that follow may be that you'll be a better mother if you do.

Particularly if more than one person is involved in initiating a document, it could be that the messages in it conflict. Sunday supplements where advertisements for garden barbecues are juxtaposed with colour features on Ethiopian famine are a dire example.

It is a good exercise, however long your document is going to be, to write down your message in not more than three words. If it can't be expressed in this short a form, it is probably too complex!

What form will your message take?

Whatever the content of your message, its form will be affected by the type of your document. You can give the same message in a letterhead for a bakery and in the promotional brochure for the same firm but the form used will be very different. Check these elements and the way they put your message across.

- What vocabulary, sentence structure?
- What type of writing – fiction, fact, description?
- What space is available to you?
- What is the document design?
- How do different pieces of text affect each other?
- How will the typesetting and illustration brief affect the text?

David Hewson

In January 1986 a new magazine called *The Wordsmith* was launched to cater for the needs of 'people who write on a computer'. It became for a while the organ for the then nascent DTP community in this country. The man behind it was David Hewson, formerly features editor at *The Independent* and now freelance. His hope was that 'the new technology would create a more plural press. The whole trade had been run on trade secrets, but now *The Wordsmith* was saying "There are no secrets. We are all publishers now!"'

David's hope was that journalists would 'rise up and fight'. The principle of journalism is that, by making information public, one defends democracy. 'I wanted more people to produce more papers so that more was being

THE WORDSMITH

| Issue Five Volume Two | £1.50 | September/October 1987 |

WE ARE ALL PUBLISHERS NOW

said in public. So the first thing was to educate people in how to do it.'

In practice, he laments, 'the technology has been used very little to produce anything of good quality in this country'. Elsewhere, it is different. David cites examples of an excellent new provincial newspaper in Galicia in Spain, and a new daily paper in Kingston, Jamaica. The latter now has a circulation almost equal to that of the *Gleaner*, which previously held a monopoly. 'The journalists who wanted to set it up phoned me for advice one night. There simply were no Macs in Jamaica, so I told them to get on a plane to Florida and buy one there, plus a copy of Quark XPress.'

Had the same spirit been present here, he believes, it would have created a new breed of innovators, 'dozens of mini-Eddie Shahs', in the publishing field. In practice, the technology is being used to do the same, old job, just in a new way. Even there, David sees the promise not being fulfilled. 'Printed material, no matter how simple it looks, requires a lot of careful thought to make it work. You have to remember that type is to read. This is a dangerous technology to put into the hands of people devoid of taste.'

Working with writers

It is tempting to think that, because you can write, you can therefore write effectively. Beware the trap of hiring professionals to do your production work but leaving the writing to an amateur – or, worse yet, a committee of amateurs. That said, your principal aim may be to publish your own creative work, and, if so, this page will not be relevant to you.

How to find a writer

For many projects, the writer is the main starting point. If you want the lead article in your dance magazine written by a famous choreographer, then no one else will do. Otherwise, use word of mouth; spread the word until you find the right person.

If you need outside expertise, we have heard of local printing shops being happy to help with short documents such as letterheads and adverts. The Society of Authors and the National Union of Journalists have lists of writers, and your local journalist training course may know of copy writers looking for work.

How to choose a writer

You will obviously want a writer with some expertise on, and sympathy with, the subject of your document.

To check writing style and skill level, you can ask to see samples of past work. It is also usual for a writer to prepare a synopsis or outline before commissioning, and you can ask for a short test piece about your message, though you may have to be prepared to pay even if you later don't use it. Show the piece to some typical readers; if it makes the right impression on them, hire the writer.

How to brief a writer

A good writer will need to know who the reader is going to be, and a good publisher (you) will be able to explain this. Also explain what your document is and its aim. If you commission writers regularly, put together a sheet of authors' guidelines including all the above, details of your house-style (see page 49), and an outline of how you work.

Your writer will also need to know word lengths, deadlines and any turn-round times for possible rewriting.

If you are using a DTP system, check whether your writer can write on technology compatible with your own. If not, it may save you a great deal of money and time to find a way they can do so. We have invited some writers into the office to work on our own computer system to ensure compatibility.

Quality control

Writers will rarely go over budget, as you usually agree a flat fee, word fee or royalty (see page 55). If what you get is not what you want, resist the temptation to do it yourself. Ask for a rewrite and/or get yourself a good editor.

Surya Lovejoy

Surya Lovejoy is a well-known journalist who writes about computers. His work appears regularly in several magazines and he also writes product manuals as well as occasional brochures and leaflets on non-computer subjects.

Given that he writes about computers, it is not surprising that he should choose to do his writing on one. He has been using word processors of one sort or another since he started his career, and his writing strategy has developed to fit the technology.

Surprisingly, he does not use the available technology of outliners or databases to prepare articles. Rather, he starts in the bath. 'I don't consciously think about it, but the bath does give me the space to conjure up a clear picture of my reader. Once I have that, and know what I'm writing *about*, I'll start writing.' Rather than write to a real person, he'll create a 'fictional individual who is a composite. I'll think "he's running a business like Fred's, has an attitude to computers like Mary's" and so on.'

Surya also needs to know how much detail his reader is going to want on each particular bit, a factor that is determined by whether they are reading out of genuine interest, or for purely utilitarian reasons such as to help them make a buying decision. Finally, he cannot start writing until he has a title for the article, and a strapline – the sentence or two that goes at the top of the article and explains what it is about.

Once he comes to the keyboard, Surya will usually start writing without any further preparation such as making notes. However, he won't necessarily write in sequence. 'I'll explain a point and think "hold on, this needs to come earlier", cut it from where it is and paste it back into the earlier section.'

Surya does a great deal of his work for computer magazines, and contrasts the way that a magazine is read with radio, where one has no choice other than to listen in sequence. 'In a magazine, people typically won't read the whole article. For example they may just scan the subheadings, or only read the summary.' He often puts information supplementary to his main article in boxes or tint panels, to give information to different levels of reader. 'My main reader is intelligent and informed, and already aware of at least one benefit of whatever I am writing about. I'll also write a "bring them up to date box" for someone who's the same type of person, but has no information about the subject. And I'll typically do an "experts' précis" box that uses more jargon and approaches the topic at a higher level.'

Although many of his readers are motivated by exclusively utilitarian criteria, Surya himself simply enjoys learning. 'I love finding out about things, and talking to people about what I've found out. Writing is just another way of doing that.'

Writing yourself

For many people, the motivation to publish comes directly from the motivation to write.

If you are writing as well as publishing, set up some feedback to make sure that you are getting it right. This could come from a disinterested potential reader, or maybe other people working on your project. You should certainly get someone else to edit your work (see page 48 on). If you are involved in creative writing, joining a local support group or writing circle is a good way of getting quality control.

We have often been asked if publishing only your own work is not in fact self-indulgent. If you are self-publishing in order to pass around your work to friends and family, it may be indulgent, but it is also very rewarding. Don't expect to sell vast numbers; do make sure you have the money to cover costs. Very, very occasionally, if you get your distribution right, the whole project can achieve success (see Joseph O'Connor's profile in Chapter 12).

Writing strategies

Strategies for writing vary, but we have found some elements that were common to every successful writer we talked to.

- Identify with your reader. As when planning your publishing venture, write for an individual whom you know, not an abstract concept of who your readership should be. Step into their point of view, ask what they need to know, how they want the information presented, and what your message to them is.
- As always, check what works and what doesn't. Get examples of successful and

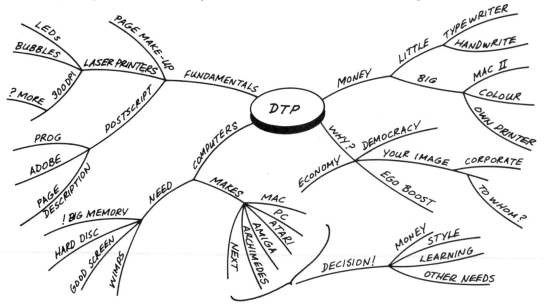

Mind maps are one way to organise your initial ideas.

not-so-successful text, and check how other writers handle things.

- Brainstorm. Alone or with interested parties, make a note of everything you feel needs to be said in your document, using a list or 'mind map' if you are paper-bound. There are also computer programs (outliner packages) for this stage in the process (see pages 46 and 148).
- Do your research. For a letterhead, this may be simply checking the postcode. For a handbook on your hobby, you may need to use specialist organisations, back copies of newspapers, face-to-face interviews with experts. Your local library may be your best resource here.
- Take copious notes. It is important to write to length, but it is easier to précis too many notes than expand too few.
- Organise. Documents that work always present their information in a well organised, and therefore easily accessible, form. Try: main idea plus information (as in a poster); different ideas linked by a common theme (community magazine); single statement (letterhead, business card); central theme developed throughout (book, leaflet).
- Work in chunks. Don't just mentally cut your book or brochure down into chapters; each paragraph, even each sentence, must have its own unique point to make, or it is not worth publishing.
- Find a hook. In every document there should be a 'hook' that will draw in the reader. If this hook isn't the illustration, make your words – the title, the slogan, the punch line, the company name – really grab attention. Headlines should be simple, direct, involving, active.
- Choose your language. What kind of vocabulary would your reader respond to? Short or long words, simple or complex, formal or informal, perhaps a particular technical vocabulary?
- Choose your word flow. Do you need long, complex sentences that explain or inform? Or short ones, to excite?
- Choose your format. Some are obvious – a letterhead or business card, for example. For longer documents, consider what length of paragraph you will use, the use of bullet points (as here) or checklists. You may want to include quotes from others, interviews, extracts of poetry, brief anecdotes, things to do. You may also need specific formats, such as a form to fill in, an order slip or an invoice.
- Write to length. A good editor can cut your work to size, but doing it yourself saves the heartbreak of seeing your best and favourite paragraph chopped. If you work on a computer, type into a structured page that will indicate when you are over-length.
- Check what you write as you go. Read your work through, checking that it makes good sense, follows any house-style and gives the right impression. Check any tricky spellings, using the *Concise Oxford English Dictionary* to back up any spelling or grammar checker you may have on your software.
- If you have one, use your editor to the full. As one of our favourite writers says, an editor is someone who 'tells me what I really wanted to say in the first place'.

Writing technology

Some writers find that they cannot use the new technology – because they are not computer comfortable or because they feel that writing is a personal issue and using technology makes it impersonal. However, computers can be extremely useful for writers.

Outliner packages

Outliner packages provide a hierarchical or 'tree' system of entering material into a file. You might, for example, wish to create one 'branch' for each chapter of a novel, with subsidiary 'twigs' to hold the different events covered, details of character, notes on conversation or landscape. They allow you to enter material at any level of organisation, and then swap levels – for example, go from one chapter or section to another – easily and quickly. Some word processing programs now have built-in outliners, others take outliner files as a starting point; they do seem to us to be an obvious, first stage for a writer collating information for a document of any kind.

Word processing programs

Word processing allows you to rewrite quickly and easily. It enables you to make 'global' changes, that is ones throughout a document; when for example you find that instead of 'Eliot' you really meant 'Elliot' , a few key strokes can correct it throughout a 400 page document. You can print out the final version of your work only when you are happy with it, and of course get good quality printouts (always a morale booster when writing).

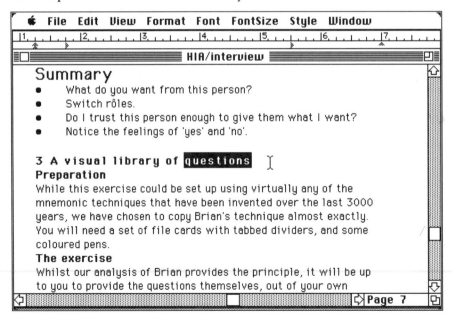

Word processing package Write Now

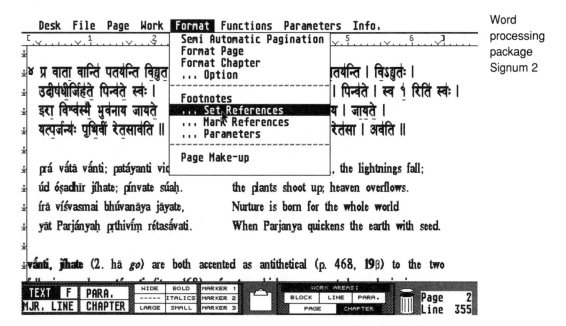

Every computer system you can buy will have one or more word processing programs available, each with their own pros and cons. It is best if you (or your writers) are using a system that works with any technology you are using for your publishing. If not, you may need to re-type in the text, transfer it electronically from one system to another, or scan it in with an optical character reader. For more on these see Chapter 8.

If you plan to use word processed text directly for typesetting (see Chapters 7 and 8), then bear this in mind when writing (or brief your writer carefully about) your house-style. Decide on clear guidelines as to how text should be typed in. Some packages will not transfer happily unless you type text in without bolds, italics and so on.

You can also set directly from word processing packages – the most recent Dirk Gently novel from Douglas Adams was written via a Mac word processing package and set directly, text formatting and all. Top-level word processing programs now carry many features previously exclusive to DTP, so the distinction between word processing and DTP is no longer clear-cut.

Spelling and grammar checkers
We cover these in detail as editing programs (page 51 on) but they are also useful to writers, because they help you tidy up work before submitting it. Many checkers have a thesaurus facility as well, to allow you to suggest words when you are at a loss for them. Never rely on checkers to replace your ability to structure language or make your work totally clean.

Working with editors

There are three main editorial jobs, though they may be called by different names in different publishing houses, and many editors combine all three jobs.

- The managing of a document: developing the philosophy of the project, finding and choosing staff, commissioning articles, checking progress, giving final approval.
- Copyediting: making any changes necessary to the text, rewriting if necessary, cutting to length.
- Proof-reading: checking for spelling or typing mistakes (literals), and for any inconsistency in wording or layout.

Finding an editor

You will probably be your own commissioning editor, although it is always a good idea to get someone else to do your 'text' editing (that is, copyediting and proof-reading) for you. Someone who uses words every day and is at ease with them, such as an English teacher, librarian or secretary, may be happy to help on an amateur basis. The NUJ or the *Publishers' Freelance Directory* will give you the names of qualified freelance professionals; try also the small ads in *The Bookseller* magazine.

Choosing an editor

Commissioning editors commission the text and manage the editing process. So if you do employ someone in this role, ask yourself whether you could work with and for them. Check their previous experience of managing projects, note whether they have sympathy with your aims.

For text editing, get candidates to edit a test piece. Does it read better because of their edit? Does it fit the word length you asked for? A copyeditor also needs people skills (for when they deal with authors whose work they have just slashed by half), while a proof-reader needs an immaculate eye for detail. The best one we know wakes up at night in a panic if he has missed a literal!

Briefing an editor

Commissioning editors, who will start the project with you, will need a contact list and lots of information about former projects. Copy-editors need information about house-style (see page 49), deadlines, and the level of freedom you are giving them to alter the wording.

Quality control

All the usual 'quality control' issues apply to editors. Pay rates for different editing jobs vary; the NUJ can give you guidance. If you don't like the work an editor is doing, or spot proofing mistakes, check that she has clearly understood your house-style before changing to someone else.

Editing strategies

Commissioning

A large part of a commissioning editor's job is identical to that of anyone organising a publishing project – creating a cohesive document that reflects the message.

Encouraging people – often a variety of people – to write is also vital, and particularly difficult in something like a newsletter, where the same people may want to hog the limelight month after month. Keeping people to a deadline is also tricky.

You must be able to say 'No'. If the article on lesser spotted warblers is not suitable for the magazine, it is not suitable. Stick to your guns.

Copyediting

The main part of copyediting is to clarify the text. We think the interview with Carlye Honig on page 54 gives an excellent outline of how to do this. We would add only a further strategy for actually breaking the news to authors that their work needs changing: point out first what is good about the text; identify what is not clear; make three or four specific suggestions about improvements. Every bit of this strategy is essential.

You may also need to cut text to length. One 'professional' approach to the problem from which we have suffered is to cut a whole paragraph of any article, regardless of the consequences. More sensitive ways include the following. You can cut whole points in the middle of text. Use this when large reduction is needed, and check with the author just in case you are ruining the argument. Or you can cut extraneous words and phrases, repetitions, digressions or extrapolations. Use this when less than one-tenth of the text needs cutting.

A copyeditor develops a 'house-style', if one doesn't already exist. She decides on a consistency of writing and layout within a document, and often across documents. It is used to keep not only the look of a document cohesive but also the way it reads. Unless you are working to an already existing house-style, it is probably easier to adopt one based on an accepted standard such as that laid down in the *Dictionary of Modern English Usage* (see Appendix for details).

Particularly difficult questions to consider are: use of capital letters; quotation marks; abbreviations; dates; spelling of words that have alternative spellings; when to use words and when numerals for numbers; use of hyphenation.

Alteration required	Mark in margin	Mark in text
Delete (take out)	℈ or ℈ /	Vertical stroke to delete one or two letters; horizontal line to delete more
Insert space between letter or words	#λ	λ
Leave as printed (i.e. a cancellation of previous marking)	*stet*	..... under letter(s) or words(s) crossed out but to be retained
Transpose	tr	⌐⌐ between letters or words, numbered when necessary
Begin a new paragraph	(n.p.)	[before first word of new paragraph
Change to capital letters	*caps.*	≡ under letter(s) or word(s) to be altered
Change to bold type	(bold)	⌇ Draw this wavy line under letter(s) or words(s) to be altered
Move to the left	⌐	⌐ Ditto
Insert double quotation marks	⁴ ⁴	λλ

Standard proof-reading marks

Proof-reading

The key issue in proof-reading is being able to hold constant a standard of style and notice when it is being broken. A good dictionary and a language guide such as the *Dictionary of Modern English Usage* can help you know what is correct, and, if you are using the new technology, spelling or grammar checkers (see pages 51 and 52) will also help.

Proof-reading involves checking the typesetting house-style (see page 97) and also the text for accuracy. A proofing checklist for text might be as follows.

- Check that the text has all been included.
- Check that it is accurate and conforms to the latest edited version.
- Check the accuracy of dates, addresses, telephone numbers, facts, your ISBN or ISSN number if any (see page 55).
- Check the accuracy of text references to other pages in the document and to art-work, eg 'the picture on the *left*'.
- Check spelling in text and artwork text.
- Check punctuation, doing special run-throughs for tricky elements.

It is tempting to think that proof-reading can be done successfully on screen. Certainly copyediting may be possible this way, but final proofing still needs to be done with hard copy (ie, on paper). We suggest that the kind of proof-reading suggested here occurs after typing in of text, and then again just before final printing or paste-up. The traditional editor's marks are still used to indicate corrections, and we have illustrated some with a sample of edited text.

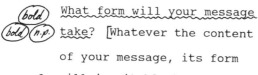

```
What form will your message
take? [Whatever the content
of your message, its form
will inevitably be affected
by the form of your
document, you can give
the same message in a
letterhead for a bakery and
in the door-to-door mailout
for the same firm but the
words used will be very
different.
```

```
What form will your message
take?

Whatever the content of
your message, its form will
be affected by the form of
your document.  You can give
the same message in a
letterhead for a bakery and
in the door-to-door mailout
for the same firm but the
words used will be very
different.
```

Left: a sample of text after editing. Right: the same text after retyping.

Editing software

If your text has been written or typed into a word processing program, there are several ways in which you can use the technology to edit it. We have to admit that we never entirely trust such programs, using them as a first line of attack and finishing up with a 'human' check at all stages. However, as a way to reduce the labour at the start of editing, they are invaluable.

Spelling checkers

Most word processing programs and many page layout programs (see Chapter 8) contain built-in spelling checkers, and there are others that can be added independently to your software range. Many of them have American spellings and usage, and you should check this before buying.

The way most spelling checkers work is that you instruct them to go through a block of text or a document, and find any word that looks suspicious. You then have the option to correct the spelling, or, in most of the more sophisticated programs, to instruct the program itself to 'guess'. You can enter into the 'dictionary' special spellings that are particular to your usage, such as trade names or technical terms, and the checker will remember them. The disadvantage of such an approach is that a word that is correctly spelt in one context may be misspelt in another. Such checkers can pick up gross errors, such as a confusion between to and too.

We find that, when working with page layout programs that divide text into boxes as opposed to those that keep the document as one entity (see Chapter 8), the time taken to

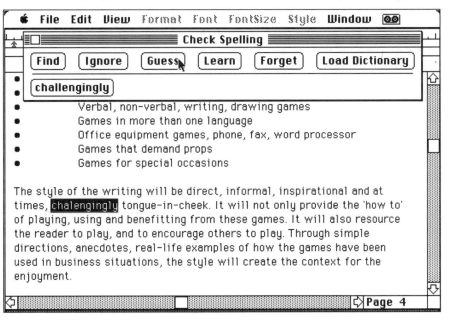

Spelling checker in the Write Now word processing package

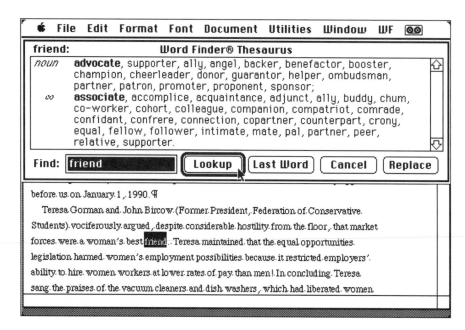

Word Finder Thesaurus package

check each separate box is counterproductive. We would therefore suggest that you use the spelling checker while the text is still entire, that is, before you drop it into separate boxes.

We would also suggest that you only allow competent editors to work with the spelling checker, otherwise you will find incorrect spellings entered and remembered as gospel by the program!

Grammar (or style) checkers

These claim to check bad writing and alert a user to it, sometimes offering alternatives, sometimes allowing you to change the wording freely.

We looked in particular at MacProof, which claims to spot unrelated sentences and structural disorganisation; recognise nominalisations and challenge whether they are relevant or not; spot the use of passive words where active words might be better; correct punctuation; recognise where language is too formal or informal; pick out easily confused words and challenge whether they are being used correctly; spot wordy or verbose expressions and suggest alternatives.

Some people love style checkers. We are wary of them, as grammar or style often needs to be flexible and subjective, and most style programs have to lay down rules in order to operate efficiently. This seems fine for what you might call the mechanics of language (spelling, punctuation); for style itself there seem so many factors to be aware of that, until style checkers become a great deal more sophisticated, we feel they may result in overproscribed writing.

For what one user called a 'clean up'

check of grammar, punctuation and offensive (ie, racist or sexist) wording, however, there would seem to be no harm in using a style checker, as long as you also proof by eye.

Word counters
Useful for both writers and editors, word counters do just what they say. You can find them in both word processing and page layout programs (see Chapter 8).

A word counter is essential for a copy or proof-reader and we would recommend you only buy word processing programs that include counters. It is extremely time-consuming, not to mention frustrating, to have to change programs to do a word count, particularly if you are cutting text and need to recheck your total every few minutes.

Be particularly wary of inaccurate word counters – some of them are horrendously so. Do take the time to read reviews, or test out the software you are thinking of buying on an already counted piece of text, checking just how far the word counter's estimate matches your own.

Other programs
There are, of course, a multitude of other programs on the market. We have found that some of the more unlikely ones can, with some imagination, be turned to good use for editing. We use a database program (an electronic version of a card file) to key in references gleaned from a book, then use its inbuilt sorting facility to reorder them alphabetically – an instant index!

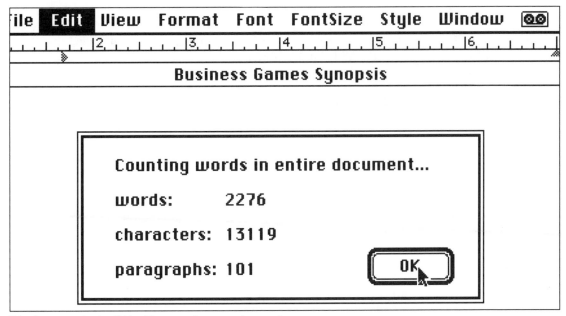

Word counter in the Write Now word processing package

Carlye Honig

Carlye Honig began work at the Exploratorium, a museum in San Francisco. She was officially a writer. 'In fact, because most of the articles were about specialist subjects, I usually ended up with an expert doing the writing – I was the one doing the editing.'

It was in this way that she began to learn her editing skills. Now, having moved to London, she does a variety of freelance copyediting work on projects ranging from serious academic journals to primary school worksheets. She loves her job.

'When something is clear, I really enjoy reading it. When it's not clear, I enjoy figuring out what people are really trying to say ... and helping them to say it.' Carlye is very emphatic that her role as editor is not to make rules and enforce them. 'There are a lot of different ways to write things. Some editors try to control their writers, be very rigid about the rules, but they are usually rules they've made up themselves.' She finds that every client she works for has developed their own house-style, and 'all of them think their way is gospel'. Carlye prefers to work very interactively with writers, aiming for clarity and respecting the author's own style.

'When I get a manuscript, the first thing I do is to read the whole thing through with my hands tied behind my back – making no changes!' If the writing is good, makes sense, is clear, she does nothing at all. She feels that some editors make changes for the sake of it, because that is their job, but 'just because it is different from the way I would do it, doesn't mean to say I have to edit it'.

Often, however, there is confusion in the writing. The main mistake authors make, Carlye believes, is to assume the reader has some knowledge that they don't have, to skip a step, or leave some key piece of information out. Her job is to notice this – 'I look for spots where I stop in the reading flow' and then clarify the confusion. She likes to work with writers, asking questions to get them to explain the full development of their argument, so that she can spot the bits they've missed out in their writing, the 'vital thing' that is the key to what they want to say.

'It's very important to act stupid at this point, to ask basic questions, to get an author to explain just what they mean.' Only then can Carlye go back and reword the confusing section so it reads clearly.

As a copyeditor, Carlye does very little basic proof-reading, though she usually checks as she goes. As a 'good speller since I was five' she has no difficulty with this, but always looks up anything she's not sure of.

The key to her copyediting skill, in fact, seems to us to be her questioning mind. She doesn't simply take rules and apply them, but reads with openness, aware of when she is confused, willing to go back and ask questions until she clears up the confusion – for herself and other readers.

Rights and wrongs

These brief notes are on some formal aspects of dealing with text. For further information see the current *Writers' and Artists' Year Book* or join the Society of Authors or the Publishers' Association.

Copyright

Copyright protection for your work is available under the provisions of the Universal Copyright Convention by printing a notice on or near the title page reading 'Copyright © ' followed by the name of the author(s) and the year of first publication. (You should probably also add further dates of publication when you reprint.) Then anyone who wishes to reproduce part of your work (other than insubstantial extracts) must obtain your permission and you are entitled to ask for payment. Your document should contain an address through which the holder of the rights can be contacted. If you want to quote from the work of other authors, you have to obtain permission from them or from their publishers. Copyright protection usually lasts until the end of the fiftieth year after the author's death.

Contracts

We have stressed throughout this book that written contracts of employment stating fee, deadline and work to be produced are vital in publishing, both for employer and employee. Publishing is in this respect a 'soft' profession; very often the fees agreed are negotiated and renegotiated according to what feels fair rather than to a fixed rate. Adapt your contract to the job in hand. If you are commissioning a short article for your local parish magazine at a cost of £30.00, then a simple letter will suffice as a contract. For book-length works, standard contracts do exist which tie up all the legalities of writing, and advice on this can be obtained from the Society of Authors or the Publishers' Association.

ISBN

You need an International Standard Book Number (International Standard Serial Number for some magazines) if you are publishing a document that falls into the category covered by this numbering system. Write to the Standard Book Numbering Agency (address in Appendix) to request registration; they will advise you whether you need to register and send you details of their requirements.

Libel

If you say anything derogatory and untrue about anyone in your publication, then you are guilty of libel. This can affect you even if you are not the writer, so as the publisher you need to take equal care. Any work that may be thought to refer to living persons should be checked before publication by solicitors specialising in the law of libel, since the cost of defending a libel action can be huge.

Royalties

Royalties are a regular percentage of the income from a document received by the publisher and paid to the author. The percentage varies but usually hovers around 10 per cent, and is often paid six monthly, on the previous six months' income. For further details about paying royalties, consult any of the professional associations.

6 GETTING THE PICTURES

Of all the work involved in producing a document, the area you may be least tempted to do yourself is the illustration. It will normally be more effective to use already existing work or find a trained artist. (We use the word 'artist' in this chapter to include photographers and computer graphics artists.)

However you will almost certainly be making decisions about illustrations – whether to include them, where to put them, what style to choose. This chapter gives some guidelines; in particular, we offer you illustration samples through which you can develop your own decision-making strategies.

Do you need illustrations?

Some documents just do not need illustrating, even though ones that don't have artwork in the text often have it on the cover. This is often due to convention (adult novels do not have illustrations) and is sometimes due to the subject matter (philosophy books have fewer illustrations than bird-watching books). If illustrations add something to your document, use them. If not, don't. This 'added something' might be:

- Giving information: maps, diagrams, step-by-step cartoons, exploded views, cutaways all give information that would be very difficult to explain. Is the information you need to convey better expressed in illustrations than words?
- Creating realism: does the use of illustrations give your reader an accurate picture of what something or somebody looks like?
- Stimulating emotion: the words may perfectly describe your line in cuddly toys, but a picture of a baby playing with one will raise emotions no words can.
- Establishing an identity: an illustration of your product can help a buyer or client to recognise what you offer. Another use of illustrations to create identity is a company logo (see page 58).
- Raising interest: if your document needs breaking into small sections for easy reading, illustrations dropped into the text will provide an effective and attractive layout.

Finally, can you afford illustrations? Commissioning them and paying for special production costs can add considerably to your bill. But if you know your document will not succeed without illustrations, then you do need them – whatever the cost.

Corporate newsletter

Young's Brewery is a family firm known for real ale. Its public relations is done by Capital Communications, run by former Fleet Street journalists Marion and Michael Hardman. They thought a corporate newsletter would 'make everyone – employees, publicans, drinkers and shareholders – feel part of the wider family. ' Young's agreed, and so *Ram News* was born.

Michael knew from the start that he would publish in-house, on an Amstrad. He already had contacts with Typeshare, a typesetter with a wide range of services including a direct setting program called Amset. 'For a few hundred pounds,' said Nick Voss-Bark of Typeshare, 'we were able to give Michael the program, the manual and a Helpline service for when he hit problems.'

Michael hit very few problems doing what he calls 'blind man's DTP'. He added Amset codes to his word processed text to indicate that 'H8, F13, M10 meant 8 point Century Schoolbook Bold across 10 picas', dropped it in to Typeshare and got page layout text back within a few hours.

It was not all smooth running. Michael developed a system of tracking how he was laying out each page by using graph paper to mark down the results of his computer codes. And he is the first to admit that his prior knowledge of typesetting helped. He warns that 'a lot of desktop publishing I see out there is being mishandled ... a synthesiser will only produce good music if you're a good musician and a computer will only produce good typesetting if you know what you're doing'.

Michael had help with the illustrations from one of his partners in Capital

Winning ways

Young's beers and pubs continue to win awards — this time from CAMRA and the Evening Standard newspaper   Page 2

Eccentric radio man meets his match   centre pages
Eating Out   Page 12
Prize crossword   Page 14

From Young's Brewery   Number 8   December 1988

LOW ALCOHOL OPENING TIME

YOUNGS have unveiled their new low-alcohol bitter in time for drinkers to enjoy at Christmas.

It is called Extra Light, it comes in half-pint bottles and is the brewery's cheapest bottled beer. The price in most pubs is likely to be less than 60p a bottle.

Marketing manager David Harvey, who has been instrumental in developing the new brew, said: "We are keeping the price as low as possible to give our customers an incentive not to drink when they are driving.

"This kind of beer is more expensive to produce than standard-strength ales and lagers, but some brewers have been criticised over their pricing policies for low-alcohol beers. We want to make sure it is cheaper than our pale ale so that people feel they are getting value for money."

Extra Light is brewed in the same way as Young's Bitter and Special, and then goes through a process called reverse osmosis to remove all but one per cent of its alcoholic content by volume.

Young's pubs have been selling low-alcohol beers from other breweries for some time, and earlier this year, a prototype of the new Extra Light was tried out on the licensees and customers of 21 Young's houses.

More than 450 customers filled in a questionnaire, which showed that 93 per cent welcomed the introduction of a low-alcohol beer and 65 per cent preferred a bitter to a lager. Only 18 per cent drank low-alcohol beers regularly but 44 per cent did so occasionally.

Communications who is a graphic artist. When it came to photographs, Michael admits to 'looking at another firm's magazine and finding to our horror 17 pictures of the company chairman in 12 pages ... we got it down to 3 in 16 pages!'. He is equally restrained when it comes to colour. 'We use spot colour from time to time, but have only ever used four colour for a photograph when the Queen Mother popped behind the counter of one of the pubs and pulled herself a pint!'

For production, on the laid out bromides, Michael pastes up his line work, marks up his photographs for the printer, and sends them off for the 13,000 print run.

Is it working? Young's Brewery seems to think so – and so did the British Association of Industrial Editors, who gave *Ram News* their 1989 prize for best company news magazine.

How many illustrations?

Obviously your aims in having illustrations in a document will affect the number you have. Illustrations meant to 'break up' a document will probably appear on every page, while those to give information will appear only where that extra information is needed.

The number you choose may well make a statement about your viewpoint. A single large portrait of the author of a book will have a very different effect from several, smaller portraits of the people in his life.

Think too about your budget; if it is limited, you may need to choose between more, smaller illustrations and fewer, bigger ones.

What should you illustrate?

Once having decided to include illustrations, you next need to go through your text rigorously and decide just what to illustrate.

- People: if the central point of your document is a person, then you may want to include an illustration of that person. Only do this if you can obtain an already existing photo or drawing, if you have a talented portrait artist to hand, or if you have a good budget for photography. Nothing looks worse than a bad photo or drawing of a real person, particularly as the full effect does not become apparent until the document comes back from the printer!
- Objects and places: here you have far more chance of good illustration because illustrations of objects and places can successfully be far more impressionistic than those of people. If you need realistic illustration, consider using library photographs.
- Cartoons: these can have a bad name in personal publishing as they are so often used as 'fill-ins', without any real sense of relevance to the text. Ideally used, cartoons can: add insight that is not given in the text itself, create humour, tell a story, illustrate a step-by-step method, or create a linking motif throughout the document.
- Maps: these can be done in several styles, from very formal to extremely humorous, and can include address, directions or travel instructions.
- Technical concepts: perspective drawings, exploded views, charts, diagrams, histograms, abstract representations of all kinds need a technical illustrator, or good reference material and a high-quality graphics package. Beware of making technical drawings so 'artistic' that they hide the information they are meant to give. Remember to include a key and clear captions.
- Logo: if your document is making a personal or corporate identity statement, you may want to include a logo. This goes on all stationery (letterheads, compliments slips, invoices, order forms) and can also be used to head up brochures and sales material. Choose one that is suitable for all these, that can be adapted for future possibilities, and that can be used in a variety of forms – different colours, sizes or positions for example.

Typeshare *SimpleSet*

SimpleSet

User Micro — Via Telephone — Mail Box — Via Telephone — Typeshare

Setting returned

SimpleSet is the latest service from Typeshare, London's first and most professional typesetting bureau. SimpleSet enables you to produce your own phototypesetting with little or no capital outlay and minimal running costs.

Using your existing Word Processor or Micro Computer, the text to be typeset is keyed in. In conjunction with Typeshare's SimpleSet Manual, simple codes are entered. These instruct Typeshare how to set your text - what Typeface, size and width to use.

The text files complete with commands are then sent to Typeshare using an Electronic Mail Box facility, such as "One to One." Within the file is a code which instructs Typeshare when to process your job and how to return it to you, be it by post, our own Couriers or collection, enabling you to achieve a very fast turnaround. Alternatively, compatible discs may be sent to Typeshare for processing.

Although designed around simple codes, the Typeshare system is very powerful and will perform many sophisticated typesetting techniques including Tabular work, Accents, Superior and Inferior Characters, Rules, Kerning and Character Pair Kerning.

Whether it's a busines card or a book you want, just SimpleSet it!

SimpleSet Offers:

● Top Quality Photosetting
● Choice of 1000 Typefaces
● 4.5 to 72 Point sizes
● Simple Operation
● No training required
● Next day delivery nationwide
● Our own courier delivery in London
● No capital outlay
● Low running costs
● Complete control
● You pay only for the work produced

Typeshare

Typeshare is the nationwide typesetting bureau.

THE ...AS BIRD

...urkey or goose, is more ... the most popular stuffing

...ieties, are delicious additions to the festive meal.

...h women will find themselves in the kitchen this Christmas.

...nake the stuffing, 73% believe that it is a women's job to stuff the turkey! ...' excuse!!).

...c, including almost as many men as women, claim to enjoy stuffing poultry.

STUFFING THE ...HRISTMAS STOCKING

CHANGE OF ADDRESS

Andrew Mortlock

72 Laing Close, Hainault, Ilford, Essex IG6 2UQ

Telephone: 01-501 3588

The choice of illustrations will be determined by what your document is about. The Typeshare sample uses a stylised flow-chart to give a technical but simple feel to the brochure, while the Christmas cookery leaflet uses cartoons to echo the light and humorous text. The inspiration for the change of address card is a traditional engraving which creates a dignified and elegant style.

What size should the illustrations be?

Here are some obvious questions to ask.

- Where will the document normally be viewed from? A poster needs larger illustration than a business card does.
- What lighting will you have? A restaurant menu, for example, is often seen in very dimly lit surroundings.
- What level of detail is needed? An exploded view of an engine must be big enough for the parts to be seen.
- What else needs to go on the page? A logo on a letter head must be small enough to allow the letter to fit on the sheet!
- What relationship is there between illustration and text? One illustration and another? A large picture of the boss surrounded by smaller pictures of the employees will make a different statement from one large picture of everyone in the firm.
- What impact should the illustration make? Usually, bigger is more noticeable.
- What size is your page layout grid? Size illustrations to fit your template divisions, creating interest by having some fit across more than one column.

Where do the illustrations go?

Positioning illustrations can be crucial. Here are some things to consider.

- How near do you need illustrations to be to the appropriate text? In the same chapter, on the same page, next to the text?

- Do you need illustrations in a particular position in relation to the text? If you want people to look at a diagram before reading the text, place the diagram above, and vice versa.
- What shape does the illustration need to be? Most are rectangular, but the dimensions can vary; strip cartoons, for example, will need a long section, maybe across a page. Given the possibilities of some page makeup packages to 'flow round', you may choose not to keep to rectangular shapes for illustrations.
- Are you choosing symmetrical or asymmetrical page layouts? Having pictures in identical places on each page gives an informal feel; mirror imaging across a spread gives a more formal look.
- Are you having 'bleeds' where the illustration runs off the edge of the page? If so, don't position bled pictures on a corner, as they look odd. Equally don't just use one bleed, but several, otherwise it will look unusual and out of place. Check that other illustrations on the spread are not visually affected by the bleed; watch out particularly for awkward, white margins.

Bearing all these points in mind, we suggest that, when designing your document, you experiment. You may be using computer layout programs or roughing out on paper. Whichever, work out what space your text will take up and then, as we suggest in Chapter 4, draw up a number of roughs showing different numbers of illustrations at different sizes in different positions. What looks good? What works?

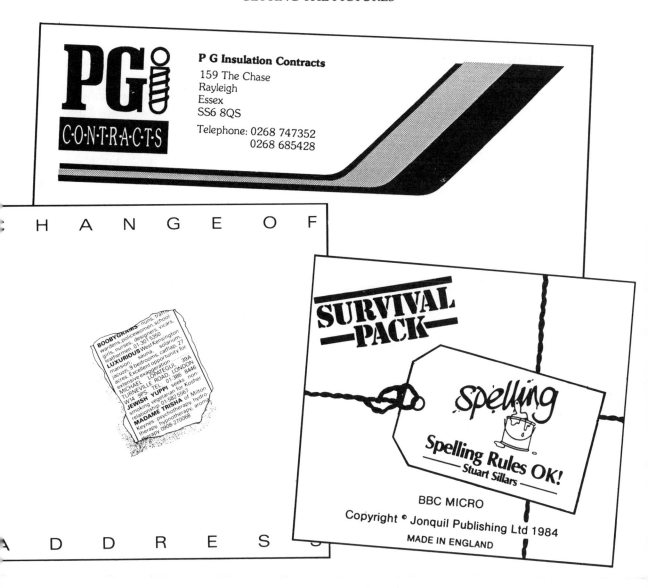

The size and placing of the illustration will affect the statement you make. On the letterhead, the illustration is placed to completely enclose the name and address. On the Survival Pack card, the illustration dominates the details. Conversely, on the change of address card, the illustration is tiny and good use is made of white space.

Should you use colour?

The following reasons are why you might use colour in illustrations – they all also apply to using colour in the text.

- To attract attention: you don't need many colours for this. One colour well used may work better – like red on a stop sign!
- To create a particular impression: bright primary colours on a poster will make a different statement to pastel shades.
- To give an upmarket feel: colour work looks and is more expensive than black.
- To create interest: even just a splash of colour, well used, can break up seemingly endless acres of black and white.
- To transmit information: a botanical drawing of a flower needs colour to give vital information about that flower.
- One of our favourite artists comments that 'colour gives a gentler impression of reality than black and white does, communicates better, gives a deeper appreciation and understanding of the text, and probably allows people to remember the illustrations more clearly'.

How?

If you decide colour is needed, think how it should be used. Do get help and support from your artist and printer on this.

If your illustration is line work (see page 64), you can use 'spot' colour, single effective blocks or splashes; you can add several colours, with several runs on the printing press. If you are using tone artwork or photographs, and want a 'full-colour' effect, you need the 'four-colour' process, which uses yellow, cyan and magenta with black to reproduce tones by printing the image in dots. We suggest that, if you are using the four-colour process, you get your printer to do the preproduction work of seperating the colours out. Remember, incidentally, that, if you are reproducing line work, your artist will present black and white illustration and you will then brief your printer as to what colours to use.

To develop your ideas, look at colour samples; Pantone is the standard colour reference system and a graphics supplier or printer will provide you with swatch sheets. Look at what works. 'Get your eye in' with three lovely books called *Designers' Guides to Colour* (see Appendix) which consist of pages of colour in various combinations.

Add colour to your layout roughs. Try different coloured papers and/or felt tip in 'spot' colour (small areas, such as rules or asterisks). Scribble in multi-colours on your rough where you think you want colour illustrations. How do they look?

Why not?

Colour costs: the preparation for reproduction is more time-consuming, and colour printing itself is costly.

Using one colour (black is counted as a colour for this purpose) is the least costly. Save money by printing some pages in one colour and some pages in another or using one colour on coloured paper. Use colour photocopiers to run through black-and-white originals masked with overlays to add colours one by one. If desperate, print in black and white and add splashes of colour with a felt-tip pen (needs a sure hand and is advisable only for informal documents).

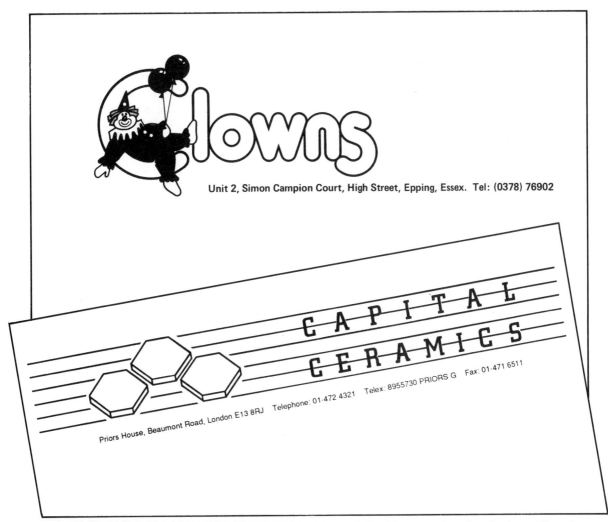

Unit 2, Simon Campion Court, High Street, Epping, Essex. Tel: (0378) 76902

Priors House, Beaumont Road, London E13 8RJ   Telephone: 01-472 4321   Telex: 8955730 PRIORS G   Fax: 01-471 6511

Despite the limitations of a book where we cannot use colour, we feel these two letterheads show different but equally effective uses of colour work. The Clowns letterhead is carried out in bright primary colours on white, ideal to reflect the image of a children's dress shop. The Capital Ceramics letterhead has a different feel: heavy pale green paper is used with green and grey ink to create a traditional and respectable look.

Drawing and painting

We use these terms to refer to any kinds of illustration that people do directly, rather than as computer art or photography.

Why human art?

The main reason for choosing drawing or painting is usually to give a more human, 'user friendly' feel. There is still the belief, whether or not you agree with it, that these media are more expressive than computer art.

Which medium?

While different artists' work will vary in style, the media they use will affect the look of the work. It is useful to be aware of this when considering what sort of illustration to commission. Some common media are:

- Ink: black-and-white ink line work is a good choice for personal publishing because it is usually straightforward to reproduce; ink washes suffer the same problems as any tone work.
- Pencil: work needs to be firm and clear in order to reproduce properly.
- Pastels and chalk: this paste of pigment and resin, which gives a soft look, is used for colour work.
- Charcoal: gives soft, gentle tones in black and white: make sure the artist uses fixative or it will smudge!
- Watercolour: as the name implies, this is water and paint. It is capable of incredibly fine washes of colour.
- Gouache: an opaque, coloured medium – useful for putting white over a dark background.

- Airbrush: gives a tonal, gradated effect.
- Acrylic or Oil: For an oil-painting look, acrylic is often faster and cheaper than oil.

It is best not to combine different media within one illustration and to take care when mixing them within one document. This book uses ink cartoons for lightness and ink drawings to illustrate processes.

Line or tone?

Line work comprises, as its name suggests, clear lines or blocks of colour, whereas tone involves shading. Line work is ideal for personal publishing, because it has very few reproduction problems. It can be pasted or scanned into your page and easily presented to the printer.

Any work that includes shading cannot be directly used for reproduction, but has to be 'screened in' in some way that reduces it to a number of small dots. This is not in itself a problem, but will add time and cost to the work. Alternatively, ask your artist to use dry transfer tint for shading (see page 79). This is made up of dots and so avoids these problems.

If you are using any colour or any work that involves shading – in effect this means anything but line ink work – check the production process before you finally decide. If you are photocopying, avoid anything but ink and do a trial run to determine how dark you need to set your contrast.

If you are printing, check with your printer first and, if it will not be too expensive, get him to do 'printer's proofs', a test run of your artwork to show how it reproduces.

Different styles of line drawing for different purposes. Charcoal, used for the drawing of the elephant, gives a soft, natural line, while ink gives more definition and detail in the architectural and technical illustrations.

The clip art on this and the facing page were originally supplied on disc. On this page, the illustration is in PostScript format (see page 152) which makes it suitable for more expensive reproduction methods such as laser printing (see page 112). The examples on page 67 are bit-map graphics (see page 142), a form of presentation most suitable for lower-cost reproduction such as dot matrix printers (see page 155).

Clip art

Copyright law forbids you to 'borrow' any pictures or words you like. There are, however, exceptions to this rule. One artist we know points out that it is not illegal to trace work as long as you change it as you go. We think that, unless you are a good artist, this may look like a bad compromise.

Copyright-free illustrations, known as 'clip art', are available in paper and computer form, and have a number of advantages. The main ones are speed and cost. Once you have tracked it down, there is nothing quicker than clip art, whether on paper or disc. Paper clip art comes in books or binders, available from any good graphics shop. Scan it into your page layout program (see Chapter 8) or paste it into your master (see Chapter 9). Letraset and Mecanorma do symbols, signs and clip art of people and trees (see page 79). Computer clip art comes in a number of formats (bit-map/object-orientated; high/low resolution; PostScript and non-PostScript; for details see Chapter 8).

Some clip art is very cheap, the cost of a book or disc. There are clip art 'clubs', regular updates of graphics on paper or disc available for an annual fee. Much computer clip art is free, made over to the public domain and distributed through friends, computer user clubs, specialist companies. It is often 'shareware'; you get it for free, and pay only if you use it. We like this approach for its basis in mutual trust.

Some people feel that clip art lacks the freshness of art specially produced for the occasion. However, it does add a professional feel, and unless your readers are 'design snobs' can be a good short-cut to illustration.

Photography

People use photographs where they want an accurate record or representation of something. Any document that wants to show that something exists will use a photograph, as will one that wants its reader to identify with the people involved. If you want to show a piece of equipment being used on the factory site; to prove to your customers that the hotel rooms are worth staying in; or to persuade electors you are a credible person to vote for, you will use a photograph.

Nothing looks less realistic – and more offputting – than poor photography in a document. We would advise you very strongly to go for the best in this respect. Resist the temptation to do it yourself unless you are already a good photographer. Don't include already existing, but rather dated, photographs. Hire in professional expertise.

If you lack time, photographic libraries are a short-cut to obtaining photographs, but, because they are mostly used by professionals, they are not cheap. However if you do need instant access to well-taken photographs, *The Writers' and Artists' Year Book* has a substantial listing of such libraries. They will need to know the subject of your photograph, what parameters you have around the photograph you need, and whether you want colour. Go in person if you can; getting them to do the work will entail you in a search fee.

Because photography is particularly useful for accurate representations, make sure that your photographs are accurate. When briefing a photographer, be clear about what you want, showing references if possible. If using library photographs choose carefully.

If a photograph should contain details you don't want, and there are no copyright problems about altering it, you can retouch. This can be done using traditional methods, but the new technology offers other possibilities. If you scan your photograph into your page (see page 156), you can alter it on screen, lightening, darkening or erasing as you wish, although quality is still a problem.

Once you have your photographs, you need to be aware of the problems of reproducing them. Photographs are made up of continuous tone, which does not reproduce easily. Photocopying photographs directly will result in very poor quality reproduction; you have to make a 'screened' version. As we explain in Chapters 9 and 10, this can be done by scanning, or by getting a graphics service or printer to screen them for you.

Decide too whether you need colour work or not. It isn't a necessity; in some documents, black and white can give just the right effect. If you do need colour work, check prices, as both origination and reproduction can be expensive. If you are reproducing colour photographs, you will be using the four-colour process and therefore you will need colour separations; we suggest you ask your printer to do these.

Particularly in the case of photographs, check requirements with your printer as you plan your document. Some types of paper (for example, newsprint) will result in poor quality reproduction; some printing processes will not do your photographs justice. It may, for example, be better to give your printer colour transparencies rather than prints; knowing this in advance will make your life a lot easier.

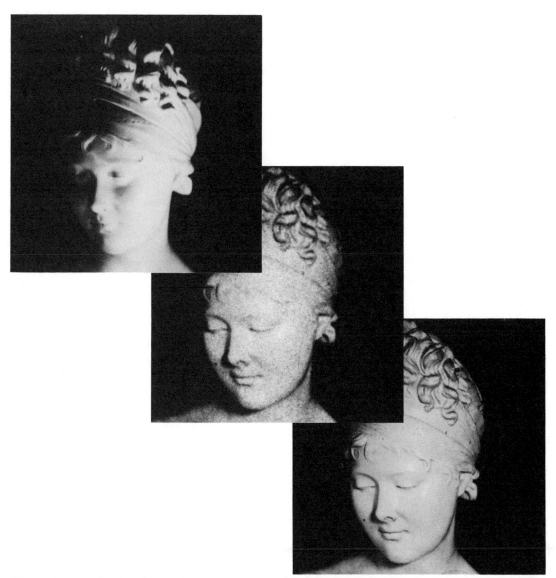

Three photographs showing the same subject treated in three different ways. The sharp focus treatment gives the most detail and is the most useful for conveying accurate information about the subject. The soft focus treatment helps evoke a romantic mood, hence its use in wedding photographs. The use of grain is technically a process flaw, but it can be used to add interest in the photograph as a graphic element and draw attention away from its content.

Computer graphics

Illustrations can be produced on computer with the same skill and artistry as human art. We deal in Chapter 8 with the technical issues that underlie the creation of computer graphics. Here we are dealing with the issues around choosing computer art and using it relevantly in your document.

Why not ?

If you are not using the new technology to produce your document, the arguments for using computer graphics are greatly reduced. Unless you are writing about computers and wish to have some relevant accompanying graphics, or have easy access to a system or artist who specialises in computer art, then you will probably stick to other media.

Equally, there is still a feeling among some people, particularly traditional designers and illustrators, that computer design lacks a human touch, that it is overstylised and hence not quite credible. If you are producing your document for a traditional market, you will probably choose not to use computer graphics.

Finally, if your illustration need is for really life-like representation, of a real person or place, computer art in its current form will not be suitable.

Why ?

There are a number of very good reasons to opt for computer illustration. The first is obviously that you like it, as many people do. When done well, it can be seen as 'state of the art'. A second reason is that you already have the technology and are looking for a quick, cheap way to illustrate your document.

Particularly if you are using a simple logo, which you can draw up yourself, then using your system for graphics as well as text can be an ideal solution to the illustration issue.

If you want something a little more ambitious, and have the time to spare, or the money to hire in expertise, then you can go a stage further. There are numerous effects on offer in the software currently available: paint effects; draw effects; the ability to distort pictures; create 3D images; zoom in on one particular area of an illustration; rotate, skew and slant images; all these can be done with graphics software. The result may be slightly abstract or streamlined, maybe with a futuristic feel, but can be stunning.

If you need accurate technical drawings, particularly in fields where computer-aided design is common, such as architecture, then computer art will be a natural choice for you. You should use one of the many graphics packages, or hire an artist with specialist expertise.

If you are illustrating tables, pie charts, graphs or similar data, computer representation is the obvious choice. In some spreadsheet packages, for example, you can key in the figures for the year's cash flow, and then with a few key strokes or mouse movements (see page 101), the program will convert these into easy-to-understand graphics that are ideal for illustrating your report or accounts.

An added bonus to all computer art that you use within your own computer system is that, in a way that is almost impossible with other forms of illustration, you can easily alter your design for future issues of your document, or if your needs change.

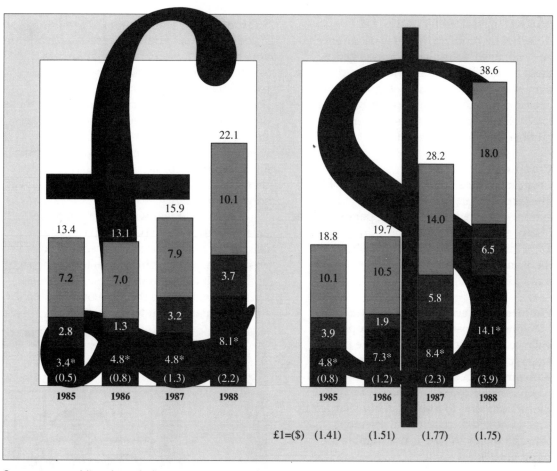

Computer graphics of yearly figures produced in Aldus Freehand, a graphics package. Fitting the various graphic elements together in this way would be beyond the abilities of the spreadsheet program from which the figures originally came. Note that the '£' and '$' signs were simply typed from the keyboard. The fact that they are so large does not mean that they had to be drawn separately.

Making illustrations fit

A particular problem that may occur once you
have obtained your illustrations is getting
them to fit. Some artists prefer to work larger
than 'same size'; often a photograph you have
obtained through a reference source will have
totally the wrong proportions. There are a
number of things you can do.

Cropping

Cropping means taking off the edges of an
illustration to make it fit or to take out
extraneous detail. Place tracing paper over the
photo, and trace the area you want to show.
Tape the marked paper over the photo and
the printer will reproduce only the area
marked.

Photocopying enlargement or reduction

Machines in most instant print shops will
enlarge or reduce line work for the price of a
single photocopy. You will lose quality, as
with any photocopy, but, depending on the
resolution you want, this may not matter.
Reductions tend to lose detail but sharpen up
fuzzy lines. Reduction or enlargement
through photocopying is not suitable for
photographs.

Scanning enlargement or reduction

Scanning a picture into your computer system
will not only allow you to place your
illustration within your page layout (see
Chapter 8), but also alter it to fit. Enlargement,
reduction and cropping are all possible using
scanning equipment.

Subcontracting reduction/enlargement

If you want your printer to reduce artwork for
you, then use a piece of tracing paper to
'overlay' the original and draw on the
reduction you want. Remember that the
proportions of the reduction must match those
of the original, otherwise the balance of the
finished version will be wrong. Tracing a
diagonal line on the overlay from the bottom
left to top right corner of the drawing and
then marking in the reduction on this line will
solve the problem.

Similarly, if you want your printer to
enlarge artwork for you, then paste your
original to a large sheet of paper and extend
an imaginary line from bottom left to top right
of the original, out to the edge of the paper.
On this line, indicate the size you want the
finished enlargement to be.

John Fuller

To describe John Fuller as an all-round artist is somewhat of an understatement. Trained as an architect, he now moves easily from jewellery-making, through perspective drawing to sculpture. 'I've just done a 7 foot high statue for a TV programme about Hitler.'

He also loves illustrating text, finding it both a challenge and a pleasure. John has a number of styles up his sleeve: realistic cartoons, odd 'wacky' cartoons, and magazine-type drawings, with young, street-credible people, 'the James Dean look-alikes' as the author of one of John's books once commented.

When being briefed, John reckons the most important thing is to 'get clear exactly what the publisher or author wants. There is room for communication breakdown here; I try to avoid that. If they don't know what they want, then I'll give suggestions and examples.'

When working on illustrations, 'I begin by reading all the text straight through, and thinking about what's required'. John keeps in mind the space he has to fill and the positioning of what he has to draw. For the cartoons, he puts overlays over the page he is illustrating, does 'some sketches on the side' and just 'lets it come out of my brain'. If something goes wrong John will start from scratch to keep a flowing style.

For the wacky cartoons, John takes a 'warm-up period ... I draw silly things to get going ... then move to a deeper level where I generate ideas for jokes. If I draw something and enjoy it, I know it'll be all right.'

The James Dean look-alikes take more research. John will work through magazines, looking for ideas and inspiration, borrowing figures, their clothes, style, positioning. Then, he adapts the ideas, tracing on overlays, 'adapting and changing the basic image. I think about contrast – how much black and white, how much tone I need to balance each page; I think about shape, and just how each image fits with the shape of the text.'

For John, 'creativity is choosing the right images for where they are going to be'.

Working with artists

Once you have decided what type of artwork you want for your document, then you need to find it. Remember that much as you may like a photograph or drawing seen in a magazine, copyright laws apply and using other people's illustrations, even in your local non-profit-making newsletter, breaks that law.

Finding the illustrations

Sometimes it is not appropriate to hire in an artist. Instead, try these sources.

- Source books, dry transfer lettering or discs of clip art from public domain libraries, specialist companies, graphics shops or friends.
- Publicity departments of many organisations.
- If you do see a particular picture or photograph you like, write to the publisher and ask if you can use it. Offer an acknowledgement, and expect to pay.
- Photographic libraries save time but are expensive. Use them if you want a photograph of something so extraordinary (location shots of Tahiti, for example!) that you would have to pay a great deal for them anyway.

Finding an artist

As with designers, it is difficult to track down good artists if you are 'outside the system'. If your project is small and unfunded, you will need low-cost (or no cost) people, and this usually means amateurs – or people committed to your cause. Professional publishers react with horror at the thought of not using professional artists. It is obviously better to use people who know what they are doing, but, if you can't afford to do so, then you can't.

Offer your document as a project to the local art college, or simply ask their graphics department for the names of their top students. We find it is a good bargain – we get enthusiasm and talent, the students get 'real work' to a real deadline. Be prepared for some disasters – but you may well end up with the next generation's David Hockney designing your poster. We extended this idea, as mentioned in Chapter 4, by placing a permanent ad in the careers newsletter of our local art college. For professionals, ask the Association of Illustrators or the British Institute of Professional Photography, or use *The Writers' and Artists' Year Book* (as always).

Choosing an artist

When you meet artists, they should bring with them a portfolio for you to view. Warn them of any special requirements you have so they don't bring along work that is irrelevant to your needs. When you do see the portfolio, go very much on your gut response. If you don't believe a particular style will convey your message, it won't.

You can ask for a test piece – though be prepared to pay for it if you don't use the artist. When you get it, do a rough paste-up (see Chapter 9) to check if the style suits, the size fits and the brief has been followed.

Finally, a word on price. Artists don't have standard rates in the same way paper merchants do, and choosing an artist means briefing her (or him) before you decide to employ her, so that she can quote accurately.

Briefing an artist

An artist will need to know what your message is and who is your market. Be clear too just which of her styles you are asking for.

For each illustration give an accurate sizing and an indication of where it is to be placed in the document. Discuss whether the artist is going to present her work 's/s' (same size) or whether you will need to budget for reduction. To give context, we brief illustrators after the text is written and laid out, so they have a page to work within. If this is not possible, you should at least indicate what text goes with the artwork.

If you are not the writer, you may choose to allow that person to attend the briefing meeting or at least put together artist' s notes. Beware the writer who tells an artist exactly what pictures are in his head and expects them faithfully reproduced- it is your job to restrain the writer, and let the artist interpret.

That said, if the illustration includes any facts or words, these should be typed out accurately for the artist to copy. Equally, if the illustration is of something not easily accessible, it will save time and money to give the artist references so that she does not need to spend time researching.

Quality control

An illustrator will normally quote a price per piece of work, and should stick to this. Photographers will often charge by the day. If you change the brief mid-way through a project, then you should expect to pay more for the work done, so budget for this. Also check for the price of extras; you will normally be expected to pay artist's expenses, including travel and materials used on the job.

Of course, ask to see roughs. Check that they are what you want, what the author wants, that any details are accurate and remember to have written material proofed. Ask for changes, and approve roughs of these before the artist proceeds to finished work. For photographs, you may want to be there at each shoot to answer questions, and approve polaroid snaps before each shot is taken.

If the final result is not what you want, don't attempt to change it yourself; whitener on an illustration will give most artists a heart attack! If you have let the work get this far without objecting, then it is partly your responsibility; however, if you are truly unhappy with the results, most artists will be willing to negotiate changes.

CHAPTER 7

PRESENTING YOUR TEXT

Perhaps one of the biggest tasks you have when getting into print is presenting your text. Particularly if you are, thanks to the miracles of modern technology, doing the job yourself, you will spend a great deal of time on presentation – all against the background of knowing that it will make or break your document.

When choosing your method, then, bear these things in mind.

- What impression do you want to make on your reader? We have known community newletters lose circulation by upgrading their presentation systems, and corporate bulletins do the same when they tried to save money by downgrading.
- In particular, what resolution (accuracy and definition of type) are you aiming at? If you need something that is pin-sharp, you shouldn't be typing it out on a fabric-ribboned typewriter.
- How much money have you got to spend? Is it spendable in large amounts now or small amounts over a few years. By judicious use of our overdraft, we cut the typesetting bills of our publishing company by 80 per cent of what they were by investing in some expensive machinery

and moving all typesetting in-house.
- How much time have you got? Taking responsibility for all your own text presentation can be very time-consuming, as you are bound to make the mistakes that we all make first time round.
- How much skill have you got? You may feel that the time and energy needed to learn how to use the new technology just isn't worth it. We would like to stress at this point that given the right technology and the right support, we think it is almost always worth learning, and it can be both easy and enjoyable to do so.
- What is accessible to you? If you can't afford the technology, or if your nearest typesetter is 70 miles away, then rejoice in what you *do* have. If you can't present as immaculately as you want to, then make it up in other ways, like superb illustrations or riveting copy.

We would advise not mixing presentation methods too much. A handwritten heading with typeset text may work well. Adding stencils, an illustration with a 'Letraset' caption, and a typed postscript just to set the whole thing off is a recipe for disaster!

Julia Howard

When Julia Howard moved to Bath four years ago she decided to put her typing skills to good use by offering a typing service to local businesses. She soon realised that, since she was now being paid by the job, she would gain considerably if she were to improve her presentation by investing in a word processor.

She leased a system that used WordStar, a program that at that time was both the most powerful and the hardest to learn on the market. A bold choice, as she now acknowledges – 'at first, I thought it was going to eat me'. She not only did learn it, however, but also began to look around for ways to extend her service. She contacted Wordsmiths, a Somerset company that had devised a system of 'direct setting', that is typesetting a word processed document directly from a disc sent to them. However she found the wait for completed work frustrating. 'If you made a mistake, you had to send the disc back again. That put several more days on to the job.' She was also starting to see the limitations of her word processing system. 'The worst thing was having to feed paper into the daisywheel printer. I would be cooking dinner in the kitchen, and every couple of minutes I would have to pop next door to change the paper.'

She therefore expanded to include a complete service from initial editing and layout, right through to the production and delivery of multiple copies of even quite bulky and complex books. Increasing success enabled the lease of a new system, a Canon PC with a laser printer that would produce an adequate quality to replace direct typesetting for the production of reports and booklets. 'Now, I can't think why anyone in their right mind wouldn't use a laser printer.' Even this system has its limitations. In many ways she would like to move on again and get a Macintosh system capable of better layout than she can achieve now. However, she feels tied to local businesses who all use IBM technology. Any expansion 'has to be taken as a business decision. I'm not dealing with pin money any more'.

SUCCESS IS A STATE OF MIND

LEARN WHY SOME PEOPLE SUCCEED AND OTHERS DO NOT - USE THIS
KNOWLEDGE TO GET WHATEVER YOU WANT OUT OF LIFE

TWELVE SUCCESS GUIDES TO HELP YOU GET WHAT YOU WANT

Success is a State of Mind   Goals for Success
Leadership Skills   Fears that Block Success
Stress   Intelligence, Creativity & Success
Tools for Success
What Do You Need to Know   Time
Workaholics - Holidays   Personal Economics
A ONE-DAY INTENSIVE COURSE FOR PEOPLE WANTING TO DEAL MORE
EFFECTIVELY WITH HUMAN EMOTIONS IN YOURSELF AND OTHERS

-o-o-o-o-o-o-o-o-o-o-

I would like to attend the following Workshops - please send me a
Registration Form and further details.

ONE-DAY IN-DEPTH

Wardrobe Strategy ☐   Saturdays in February
                         LONDON and BRISTOL
Success is a State of Mind ☐   £65 including VAT

MINI-WORKSHOPS - BRISTOL - set of 4: 1 per week Feb/March

Goal Setting ☐

Time Management ☐

Text presentation options

New technology has meant that, nowadays, most people can present text typeset if they want to. In this chapter, therefore, we have devoted a great deal of space to typesetting, and in the next chapter even more space to the new technology. However, remember that if you have no computer – and have no desire to get one – you can still get into print.

Handwriting

Handwriting is the cheapest and often the quickest way to present text; used sparingly, it can look professional. Many corporate logos are originally handwritten, and it can work very well. Unfortunately, more than a few words in handwriting is suitable only for documents like party invitations and special interest posters. Anything else can look amateur.

Handwriting needs to be clear, stylish and executed with a sure touch. Employing someone who has calligraphic training will help enormously. If you do the writing yourself, use a drawing pen, which gives a constant line width, usually marked on the tip (0.2 mm, for example, or 0.5 mm). Be careful to space your letters evenly and, if you are writing in capitals, to keep the heights of the letters the same.

Stencils

There are various kinds of stencil for lettering. Rotring and Faber-Castell make good ones and cheaper alternatives can also be bought or made from special stencil card. Like handwriting they should be used sparingly and with care otherwise the effect can be unprofessional.

This is an example of handwriting in black ink.

This is an example of handwriting in black ink.

This is an example of stencilled text.

This is a heading created with dry transfer lettering

This is text created on an
electric typewriter. This is
text created on an electric
typewriter. This is text
created on an electric
typewriter.

This is text created on a
manual typewriter with a fabric
ribbon. This is text created
on a manual typewriter with a
fabric ribbon.

Dry transfer lettering

This is lettering that you transfer from a sheet on to your paper by rubbing down on the sheet – Letraset and Mecanorma are the most popular makes.

The initial outlay per sheet, though not cheap, is certainly more attainable than a computer for typesetting. The system offers every typeface you could think of, a few you never would, and is particularly good for lines, rules and tones. If you are not working with the new technology, we would unhesitatingly recommend using these rather than trying to draw letters yourself. Dry transfer lettering is easy to do, and the professional look gives an upmarket feel to your document. It is time-consuming, though, and so only suitable for small areas of text.

To do transfer lettering yourself, draw a baseline in light blue pencil for the space marks below the letters to align on, rub down with the end of a soft pencil or burnisher. Ease off mistakes with masking tape, and leave a space the width of a letter 'i' between words. Note that with all makes but Letraset, you need to assess the spaces between letters by eye.

Typewriter output

Typewriting is cheap, accessible and easy. It is high resolution, though the letters often aren't proportionally spaced so can be hard to read. Nowadays it is probably not suitable for really upmarket presentation.

Particularly if you are aiming at a 'friendly' market where overprofessionalism might in fact lose you readers, then use your typewriter and glory in it! However, if you do own a typewriter, make sure your document

This is text produced by a dot-matrix printer connected to a computer running word processing software. **Bold** and *italic* text are easy to produce. This is text produced by a dot-matrix printer connected to a computer running word processing software. **Bold** and *italic* text are easy to produce.

This is text produced by a daisywheel printer connected to a computer running word processing software. This is text produced by a daisywheel printer connected to a computer running word processing software.

This is text created on an electric typewriter and reduced on a photocopier by a factor of 2/3. This is text created on an electric typewriter and reduced on a photocopier by a factor of 2/3. This is text created on an electric typewriter and reduced on a photocopier by a factor of 2/3.

design (see Chapter 4) works within the possibilities you have available. These are likely to be one typestyle, upper and lower case. Type out all your material in columns of the width you have decided for your page. Type pagination and odd bits such as title pages, contents, indexes and illustration text separately. For errors, retype the whole line and paste it over the original copy. Cut and paste the finished work into each grid (see Chapter 9).

Word processor output

Word processed text is easier to do than typewriter text because it allows you to correct mistakes without retyping complete pages. It often gives you one or two styles of type plus bold and italic, and control over the width of text (measure) you work to. You will type in a continuous column and paste up your text when you have finished.

For word processor output, you will usually have a choice of daisywheel or dot matrix printer which are covered in more detail on pages 154-5.

Once you reach the high end of the word processor market, you are nudging the next stage, typesetting. Many machines that take word processing programs can, with a different pieces of software and a different printer, be turned into machines capable of producing typeset text laid out on a page.

For both typewriter and word processor output, one approach which many people use is to have each page of typed copy reduced by photocopier. For example, you can reduce two pages sufficiently that they fit on a single page, thus saving paper and giving a more compact feel.

Typeset text

Typeset text uses photographic images to set letters clearly. It is easy to read, allows more letters on a line, gives more sizes and styles and has a credible, upmarket image. There are many ways of getting your text presented in a typeset form.

Using a typesetter

Even five years ago, the only option for typesetting was to take it to your local typesetter, wait a long while and pay hugely.

If you do choose to go along this route, then type up your copy in one long column with large margins and 'mark it up' to instruct the typesetter how you want it set. He will return it to you for correction in one long roll called a 'galley' and will then make a final run-through to produce perfect text for you to paste up.

Direct setting

Even if you don't have page layout packages, it is still possible to get typesetting better than traditional typesetting done from your system.

One way, which cuts down on cost though still needs you to brief the typesetter, is for you to supply them with a disc. You provide your text as an ASCII file, which is a standard form of computer text. The typesetter inserts special computer codes to make the text look the way you want it to. Text still needs reproofing, and the turn-round time is not much better than that for traditional typesetting.

Some typesetters let you help. You type in the text, then add certain codes which tell the setter how to handle your text. These codes are usually simple and allow you to define different kinds of type clearly. The turn round time and the cost are lower because you are doing more of the work yourself, although you need to be able accurately to visualise the end result in order to get value for money. Mistakes cost dear; the horror of realising you have set three pages in 4-inch high text has to be experienced to be believed!

For both these direct setting methods, you need to check with a typesetter first to find out whether he can do what you want, and if so how you need to present your text.

Do-it-yourself

The DTP revolution is founded in part on the fact that you can now type in texts and see your copy as it is going to look when typeset. This is called 'WYSIWYG' (what you see is what you get).

For printing out text for presentation, you can use a low-cost printer (daisywheel, dot matrix, etc) on which you get low to average resolution or a high-cost printer (laser or equivalent) on which you get high resolution. You don't need to have a laser printer yourself; there are many computer bureaux that will run off copies for you very cheaply – as well as community typesetters and cooperative printing schemes that can help. If you need even higher resolution than a laser printer gives, then you can get typeset output on photographic paper (bromide).

Do-it-yourself text presentation, therefore, is now available to anyone who has access to the technology. But this raises a central problem: to typeset properly, you need to know about typesetting.

Typeface

Use this section not only to learn about typesetting if you are using the new technology, but also to brief your typesetter if you choose any of the direct-setting methods.

Anatomy of a typeface

The word typeface (or font) describes all the sizes and styles that make up a particular design of type. Any particular letter in a typeface has certain characteristics. These are ones it is useful to know.

- The baseline is the imaginary line on which a letter such as a, b or c stands.
- Upper case letters are capitals.
- Lower case letters are 'small' letters.
- The distance between the baseline and the top of an upper case character is called the cap (capital) height. This is usually the highest point of a font, although, in some faces, lower case letters such as l are taller than upper case ones.
- The distance between the baseline and the top of lower case characters such as a, c or x is called the x height.
- The ascender is any part of a letter that goes above the x height – the letter h has an ascender.
- The descender is any part of a letter that goes below the baseline.
- A serif is a small stroke at the end of any line that makes up a letter. 'Serif' typefaces have such strokes, 'sans serif' faces don't.

The shape of a typeface makes it unique. However, there can be many variations of a typeface, and these variations together make up a type family. For example:

- A typeface can be produced in different sizes, called point sizes. A point is 1/72 inch (12 points makes up a unit called a pica; there are 6 picas to an inch). Page 85 shows type set to different point sizes.
- An upright version of a typeface is normally the standard one; it might be called Regular, Book or Roman. A version that slopes to the right is a classic variation called Italic (Oblique for a sans serif face).
- A typeface can be produced in different weights. Medium or Regular is the standard weight, with Bold and Extra Bold being heavier, Light and Extra Light being lighter. Ultra and Semi are added in some typefaces.
- A typeface can be distorted to give different effects. Common distorted faces are Condensed (thin), Extended (wide), Outline, Underline.

A full typeface could consist of Light, Regular, Bold, Extra Bold. Each of these might be also be in italic, condensed and extended. Each could conceivably be set in any point size from 1 up to infinity, though in practice 6 point is the smallest 'recommended readable' size. Typesetters usually offer from 5 to 72 point sizes in a typeface; larger sizes are called 'headline faces'.

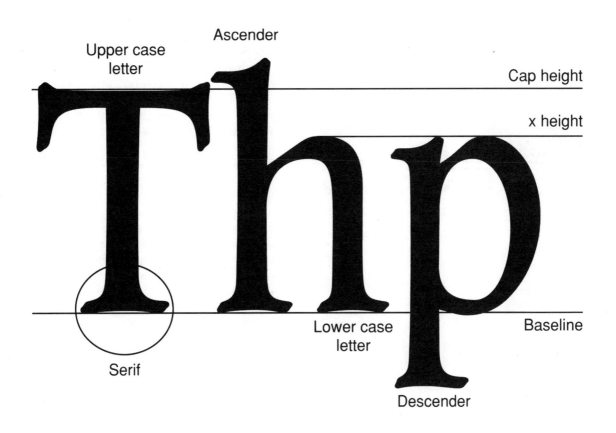

Upper case
letter

Ascender

Cap height

x height

Serif

Lower case
letter

Baseline

Descender

ABCabc
Serif face (Times)

ABCabc
Sans serif face (Helvetica)

ABCabc
Script face (Zapf Chancery)

ABCabc
Typewriter face (Courier)

Choosing a typeface

There are many hundreds of different typefaces. Look at the examples in the illustration on the left; think of these as shapes rather than letters, and become aware of the different impressions they make on you.

One of the main differences between faces is whether they are serif or sans serif. Serif faces (such as Times) tend to be seen as more traditional, sans serif (Helvetica) as more modern. Other faces are designed to have the feel of handwriting (Zapf Chancery) or typewriter text (Courier), while yet others are display faces with very fancy, special effects.

Choose your typeface carefully, bearing in mind what impression you want to make on the reader. Look as always at examples of documents you like, and find out what typeface they use. Get sample sheets (the Letraset catalogue is a good reference source).

We would recommend, incidentally, that you never use more than one or two type families per document unless you have a good reason for it. (Many of the people we interviewed confessed to using four or five when they first started publishing 'but grew out of it...'). Reasons to use different typefaces might be: for illustration material; to emphasise items on a totally different topic; for headings.

Choosing a point size

Main text for a document is usually set in 10, 11 or 12 point. Prelims, indexes, footnotes are smaller, headings go larger. Other factors count though – such as the distance your document will be seen from; the emphasis you need elements to have; the lighting in the environment, or even what emotional state

6pt Times Roman
7pt Times Roman
8pt Times Roman
9pt Times Roman
10pt Times Roman
11pt Times Roman
12pt Times Roman
13pt Times Roman
14pt Times Roman
15pt Times Roman
16pt Times Roman
17pt Times Roman
18pt Times Roman
19pt Times Roman
20pt Times Roman
24pt Times Roman
28pt Times Roman
36pt Times Roman
48pt Times Roman
64pt Times Ro
72pt Times R

readers will be in (late-night restaurants have to choose their typestyles carefully, so that tired or inebriated customers can easily read them!).

You will almost certainly be including in your document not only main text but also heads, subheads, contents list, indexes. The usual way to distinguish these is to set them in the same typeface but different point sizes and/or weights. So, for example, the text for this book is in 10 point while the main section headings are in 15 point, the subheads in 10 point bold, the chapter headings in 29 point.

If you need to check what point size text is, you can use a typescale which allows you to measure it. This is useful to do when using a computer because typesizes on printouts can vary; always print out a sample and check to see how large it actually is.

Choosing italic/oblique
These faces are normally used to 'pull out' special words, such as foreign or technical terms or book titles. It doesn't carry as much emphasis as bold, and tends to look lighter on a page, so use it with care.

Choosing different weights
The usual weight for main text is the standard (Medium, Regular) weight. Bold can be used, like larger point sizes, to give emphasis to headings or text. Beware, though, raising the point size and also adding weight. Try it out first, by testing it on screen if you have a computer, or tracing/dry transferring letters on to a rough if you haven't. The heading on this paragraph is in bold, but we have kept the point size at 10.

Roman

Bold

Italic

Bold Italic

Outline

Shadow

<u>Underlining</u>

Reversed Out

Choosing distorted faces

We would advise you not to use distorted faces, at least until you have a lot of experience. If you must, then use them only in headings. Condensed and Extended make a certain amount of text smaller or larger than it is in the standard typeface. Outline, Underline and Reversed Out give interest and emphasis, but italic or oblique is always more acceptable than either. It is possible to do these faces on many page layout programs.

Curving, slanting and reshaping text, which is possible with some software, is great fun if used in moderation for documents that need an original touch, such as invitations, advertisements or product labels. To do these yourself, you need specialised graphics programs which we cover in Chapter 8.

Choosing upper and lower case letters

If you are accustomed to using a typewriter, where one of the only available ways of emphasising words is to capitalise them, then you may be tempted to do the same when typesetting. In fact, this only really works for headings – capitals in the main body of the text look clumsy. We suggest you try capitals for headings, but avoid them for everything else.

Oversized capital letters can be used at the start of a paragraph for effect. Single letters can fall above the first line, take up the first few lines of text, be highlighted with tone in some way. A whole line of text in a slightly larger point size than the text capitals can start a paragraph.

Spacing

A well-spaced document is a pleasure to read, because the characters, words, lines and blocks of text are well placed. Too little space between them makes them hard to distinguish, too much space is distracting.

Character spacing

Typeset text has 'proportional spacing', where letters take up different amounts of space – as opposed to 'monospaced', like most typewriter text, where each letter takes up the same amount of space. Proportional spacing gives a much easier text to read, and allows you to fit much more on to a line, and hence on to a page.

Kerning

This facility, which allows pairs of characters to move slightly closer together, gives a tighter, more professional look to text.

Word spacing

When typing, the convention is to place a single space between words and a double space at the end of a sentence. With most typesetting programs, single spacing throughout works better. Double spacing can create odd gaps, particularly where you have decided to justify the type on both sides of the text and so the words have to space out to fill a line.

When using justification (see page 91), the computer may insert long spaces between words anyway. You may choose to change to unjustified text, to hyphenate words to make them flow on to the next line, or even to alter the text to prevent large gaps between words.

Monospaced font

Fractionally spaced font

Kerning

OVERSPACED

NORMAL

UNDERSPACED

LEADING

Text set with a wide line spacing has a totally different feel to it from text set normally. This style is often used in advertisements. This is 12pt Avant Garde set with 16pt line spacing. A typesetter would call it simply "twelve on sixteen".

Text set to a very narrow line spacing looks extremely cramped, and is very hard to read. This is 12pt Avant Garde with 12pt line spacing, in other words "twelve on twelve".

Line spacing

When all typesetting was done with movable metal blocks, the space between lines was created by putting in slips of lead; these spaces are now called 'leading'. When you hear designers or typesetters describing type as '10 on 12', the first figure describes the typeface (10 point, see page 82) and the second figure tells you how many point spaces there are between one baseline of type and the next.

Using white space

Developing a sense of what is too much and what is too little space between text and illustrations is the sign of a skilled personal publisher. Setting text so that the areas of white space between characters and words are pleasing is a challenge – but beware 'rivers' of white space in justified text.

Making the text fit

You need to get a good fit between text and the space available. If you are using a computer, simply key in the text and then play with the point sizes until you find one that looks right. If you are computerless, you can count the average number of characters to a line of the point size and measure you want, and the average number of characters per line in your text, then use this information to work out how many lines of text you will have.

If you then have too much text, cut it. If you have too little, rethink your document rather than simply 'padding'. Typesetting solutions such as reducing the point size rarely work as they make minimal changes to the space text takes up.

Text layout

Chapter 4 explained how a document is designed so that text and illustrations fit together in a way that is right for the document. From a typesetting point of view, there are more specific design issues to be considered where type is concerned; some of these, of course, overlap with points we have made in Chapter 4.

Margins

The space between the edge of the page and the text is the margin. Traditionally, as explained in Chapter 4, there are proportional relationships between the various margins; the important thing to remember when setting your text is that, when you look at a page or a spread, the margins should look balanced and set off the text and illustrations well.

Columns

When laying out text, arrange it in columns down the page. As explained in Chapter 4 on document design, columns can be of varying widths, aimed to make text as easy as possible to read.

Gutters

The space between the columns, or the inside margin of a page, is called a gutter. You need to balance this space with all the other margins on the page to give a pleasing effect.

Measure

The measure of a piece of text is the width each line is set to. This will correspond to the width of your columns in the template you

GUTTER

Two very narrow columns create an interesting effect at the expense of legibility.

The columns are only 33mm wide with a 6mm gutter between them.

Two very narrow columns create an interesting effect at the expense of legibility.

The columns are only 33mm wide with a 6mm gutter between them.

7.3cm

This column is set to a 7.3cm (17pica) measure - the same as the main text of the book. The bite taken out of the left hand side is created by wrapping the text around a section of a circle. It could equally have been wrapped around a picture or logo. This width is common in magazines and non-fiction books.

read your text; if your measure is too long, try increasing the margins or having more than one column. Equally, a too short measure will break up the meaning of your text into chunks that are difficult to assimilate.

Justification

Within the possible width of the measure, the text can be laid out in a number of ways. It can be arranged centred in the middle of the grid area – this is common for titles and subheads. If the text fits snug to the margin on the left, and not on the right, it is said to be ranged left. This paragraph is ranged left, a very satisfactory layout for big areas of text. Its only drawback is that if the passage is full of long words then there can be a very ragged edge on the right. If the text is snug on the right and not on the left, it is ranged right.

When both margins are straight, this is termed right and left justified (or simply 'justified'). It is a formal layout, and can cause problems with spacing. For words to fit the measure, there may need to be considerable space between them, which may look odd. To avoid this, you may introduce hyphenation.

Hyphenation

Most computers automatically insert hyphens to allow a neat-looking spacing along a line. Many have sophisticated programs which allow you a great deal of control over where words can be hyphenated. It is also possible to 'turn off' the hyphenation function if you don't like hyphens falling at the end of a line. Sometimes the program inserts inappropriate hyphens – for example, placing three at consecutive line ends, which looks clumsy. Reword the text to avoid this.

This text has been set to a very narrow (4cm) measure. We have set this unhyphenated, with the result that the right-hand margin is very ragged.

This text has been set to a very narrow (4cm) measure. By using heavy hyphenation we have been able to keep the right-hand margin quite regular.

One problem with justified text is *rivers*. These are vertical gaps in the text which occur at random and distract the eye from scanning easily through the document. They particularly plague narrow columns where hyphenation has not been used.

This paragraph could be variously described as *ranged left, left justified* or *unjustified*. All three phrases have exactly the same meaning.

This paragraph could be variously described as *ranged right*, or *right justified*. Both phrases have exactly the same meaning.

This paragraph has been centred. Centring is normally only used for headings.

This paragraph could be variously described as *justified*, or *justified both*. Both phrases have exactly the same meaning.

This paragraph could be variously described as *justified*, or *justified both*. Both phrases have exactly the same meaning. It has also been *auto-hyphenated* to reduce the *word spacing* (gaps between each word).

Paragraphs

A block of text such as a paragraph can be dealt with in various ways. The first line can start snug to the margin. Alternatively, the first line can be started slightly in from the margin; this type of space is called an indent.

Whether or not your text is indented, you could leave a line between each paragraph. Alternatively, if you wish to emphasise that the point the paragraph is making is separate from that made by the text around it, you could indent the whole paragraph. All these possibilities could be carried out with justified or ranged text.

Tabs

If you want to set text in tables or tabular form, it is important to use tabs rather than insert spaces to move the text across the page. Most programs allow you to set the position of tabs and the alignment of tabbed text.

Page division

How do you know when to divide your text to make a new page? Some page layout programs make this decision for you, breaking the text whenever it fills up a page. On other programs, you have the facility to create individual pages and then have to work out which text goes where.

Plan your page breaks carefully. In documents consisting of small articles, try to keep each article or set of articles on a separate page. When a paragraph division leaves one word alone on a line this is called a widow. When the first or last line of a paragraph or heading is left stranded by a page break, this is called an orphan. If your text falls like this, rewrite to avoid such instances.

Technical documents frequently use multiple tabs. We have used grey vertical rules to indicate where tab stops have been set in this column.

A First level tab for main point. First level tab for main point. First level tab for main point. First level tab for main point. First level tab for main point. First level tab for main point.

   A1 Second level tab for subsidiary point. Second level tab for subsidiary point. Second level tab for subsidiary point. Second level tab for subsidiary point.

      A1a Third level tab for subsets of the subsidiary point. Third level tab for subsets of the subsidiary point. Third level tab for subsets of the subsidiary point.

B Second major point also at the first level. Second major point also at the first level. Second major point also at the first level.

   B1 First of two subsidiary points to the second major point. First of two subsidiary points to the second major point.

   B2 Second of two subsidiary points to the second major point.

C ...and so on.

This paragraph has been set with an *indent*. The first line acts as if it were tabbed, but subsequent lines run the full measure of the column. Indents can be set as standard format commands.

This is the opposite effect, called a *hanging indent*. Here, the first line runs the full measure of the column, subsequent lines act as if tabbed. You might use hanging indents on a title page, as it puts extra emphasis on the first line of each paragraph.

7pt

If you measure the space between all the paragraphs in this column you will find that they are about half a line space apart. The paragraph spacing has been set to 7pts.

Parts of a document

Different parts of a document, apart from the main text, need different typesetting approaches.

Cover

The main aim of a cover is to attract attention. It also needs to be informative. Use simple, clear, usually large, typography, bearing in mind that the cover is what the reader (possibly the buyer) is going to see first. There are no conventions about positioning of text on a cover, though it is usual to give prominence to the title.

Prelims

In a book, these normally include the title page, dedication, acknowledgements, preface, contents, list of illustrations, and copyright and printing details. In a brochure or magazine, prelims consist of an abbreviated version of these. They set the style for the rest of the document, so need to pick up on the typeface and general document design used throughout.

Choose your typography for the prelims separately from that of the main book. The fonts will be the same, but point sizes may be much bigger (for titles) or smaller (for printing details or illustration lists). In the prelim pages in particular, you are likely to have long lists; you don't have to use the full measure of the page for such lists, but can set up narrow columns so that your lists don't look too spread out. If you want to link two columns, for example, a contents list with page numbers, put 'leader dots' across the page to join them.

Superscript $^{\text{like this}}$ and superscript $_{\text{like this}}$ are normally used to indicate notes[1] or create fractions such as $^3/_4$.

---

[1] including footnotes

Leader dots

Alpha.. 1
Beta 2
Gamma 3
Delta 4
Alpha.. 1
Beta 2
Gamma 3

Leader lines

Alpha ————————————— 1
Beta ——————————————— 2
Gamma —————————————— 3
Delta ——————————————— 4
Alpha ——————————————— 1
Beta ——————————————— 2
Gamma—————————————— 3

Leader dashes

Alpha -------------------------------------- 1
Beta-- 2
Gamma ------------------------------------ 3
Delta--- 4
Alpha -------------------------------------- 1

Headings

In any document, you should probably have only three or four kinds of heading dividing up the text; the main heading will be the most important, and will title the main divisions such as chapters; the others are called subheadings.

You can emphasise headings by using capitals, bold or sometimes even italic, rules or tint boxes and striking positioning. The headings in this document are Palatino 29 point for the chapters, Palatino Regular 15 point ranged left for the first subheading and Palatino Bold 10 point ranged left for the second subheading.

Headers and footers

These are words or numbers that appear on the top (or bottom) of each document page. Because they appear regularly, they will be part of the overall document design.

Sub- and superscript

These are figures or letters, usually in a smaller type size, which drop below or rise above the normal line, and are usually used for notes or fractions.

Added extras

Some items in the text may need to be expanded or cross-referenced. This can involve adding text at the foot of the pages (footnotes), at the back of the book (in appendices, notes or reference pages), in the margin (margin notes) or in a section displayed separately within the body of the text. If the addition is not near the text itself (ie, not in the margin or separate display) then indicate where it is to be added by an asterisk or superscript number and cross-reference this to the addition.

Pagination

Page numbers, or pagination, can be positioned in a number of places on a page. The standard places are: centred at the bottom of the page, or at the outer bottom or top corner. Most computer programs allow you to add your pagination automatically.

Captions

Captions to go with illustrations need a typographic style of their own. You may want to use a different weight or style, rule them off or place them obviously near the illustration.

Index

This is normally set in much smaller type than the main body of the text; and hence it usually takes up less space and is set in narrow columns. Often, the words of an index are set in normal text and the page numbers in italic, with bold being used for emphasis.

Sidebar

This is a space on the margin, often within a box or tone bar, where extra information or quotations can be placed.

Special effects

Rules and boxes

Lines are called rules in typesetting to differentiate them from 'lines' of text. They can come in various thicknesses and in various tones from light to dark; don't mix different thicknesses and tones within a document, in the same way as you wouldn't mix typefaces.

Rules can be set out to form boxes. Both are used to divide, link or emphasise text or illustrations. Both should be used sparingly – it's often far better to leave a line space or create a division by using headers than to insert a rule.

Box asterisks and other pi characters

Boxes, signs, logos such as ❂ or ●, and directory symbols such as telephones or caravans are known as pi characters. If you are not using computer software that provides them, they can be inserted using dry transfer lettering. The more exotic ones, when used as decoration on informal documents like posters or invitations, can work – or can make the documents look overdecorated.

Shades and tints

Many layout typesetting programs now provide shades and tints to be added over or behind text to emphasise it or to divide it from the main body of the document. If your program doesn't provide it, you can add it by hand as self-adhesive film. As with boxes and rules, don't overdo tint; notice that, unlike 'continuous tone' in photographs, it doesn't need screening. Tints reproduced on a laser printer are sufficiently coarse that text laid over a tint can be hard to read.

1/2pt rule
1pt rule
2pt rule
4pt rule

pi characters

10% tint panel with text

20% tint panel with text

30% tint panel with text

40% tint panel with text

Proof-reading typesetting

All text needs to be proof-read for accurate typesetting. It also requires checking for spelling and punctuation. This is usually done by a proof-reader, although it could be done by whoever is responsible for the typesetting if that is more appropriate.

All the points made in Chapter 5 about language proofing apply here. By now you will have developed a typesetting house-style and decided on a consistency of typeface, measure, point size and so on. Play with sample layouts, printing them out if you are using the new technology, then use our checklist in Chapter 3 to work out a comprehensive list of the decisions you are taking.

When you or your proof-reader is ready to check proofs, it is fine to do so on screen, but follow this by a proof of paper or 'hard' copy.

A checklist for proof-reading might be:

- Check font and point size consistency for text, headers, special styles.
- Check measure and indents, word spacing.
- Check all alignments of text and graphics.
- Check paragaph spacing, leading.
- Check for hanging hyphens, widows and orphans.
- Check all page layouts are correct.
- Check any specials – rules, boxes, asterisks.
- Check prelim pages which may have a different house-style.

When errors are spotted, mark them as you would do language errors. Some traditional marks for typesetting corrections are shown in the illustration.

Working with typesetters

If you do use a typesetter, decide first whether you want someone who can set your whole document from scratch, a bureau to run your disc through, or something in between.

Finding a typesetter

If you have a network of computer support, someone on it will almost certainly have a favourite bureau for sending through discs. Equally, if you have found a good printer, he will almost certainly have links with a trusted typesettter. Alternatively, scour your *Yellow Pages* or DTP magazines for typesetters.

Choosing a typesetter

A computer bureau that just runs your disc through its machine needs to have the right machines, a quick turn-round time and a fair degree of rapport. A typesetter who is working with your text needs to know his business. We suggest that, when using a typesetter or bureau for the first time, you give them a small and unimportant order that you don't need in a hurry. Check their track record, their attitude to your work, their timing, their accuracy and whether they understand your instructions.

Briefing a typesetter

Even for a simple run-through, a bureau will need to know well beforehand what hardware and software system you are using for your text and graphics, and whether their system is compatible. If the software isn't compatible, you should consider converting your text to an ASCII file and presenting it like this. A computer bureau will be able to give you some guidelines on how. Bureaux will also need to know how much text and graphics you are giving them before they can give you a price and schedule.

If you asking the typesetter to do any work on screen, be that typing in your text and setting it, or adding computer graphics to your document, you will need to brief him thoroughly with details of your document. If you are giving the typesetter your text on paper, you need to mark this up with the details outlined in this chapter.

Quality control

The quotation a typesetter gives you may be based on the number of words in the document, the number of spaces, the number of lines. He may charge extra for lists and tables, and will certainly charge extra if your work is badly prepared, meaning more work for him. His quotation will cover any errors on his part, but not errors or changes of mind on yours. To protect against this, ask to see a cheaper, laser printed version of your text before going on to the expensive final stage of setting. Differentiate between the typesetters' errors and any changes on your part, in different colours, so that the typesetter can see which is which.

Patrick Brown

When local directory publishers Nigel Burney and Charles Stirrup asked Patrick Brown to set them up an in-house typesetting operation, Patrick jumped at the chance. 'Charles just asked me to give him a shopping list of equipment. A week later we were up and running,' he explained. The operation, Hierographics, since renamed Alphabet Set, is now one part of the Passport Group, handling setting for outside customers as well as continuing to typeset the directories.

Patrick's background is not in typesetting. His first job after coming to this country from just outside Belfast was with Instant Office, a mailing and word processing house. There he learned to use Apple computers, and took this knowledge with him to The Graphics Factory, the first DTP bureau in the country.

He considers his lack of traditional typesetting background to be an advantage rather than a handicap. 'The people who will succeed in DTP are the ones who really care about what the client wants. A lot of traditional typesetting skills are to do with setting letters and words in the right place; skills that are no longer relevant because the computer does all that for you.' He admits,

however, that design skills are now needed more than ever. 'DTP trainers must know both design and computing. Few actually do.'

Patrick's office in a converted warehouse by the Thames at Chelsea is littered with computers. Although he has standardised on to Macintoshes, his half dozen staff use a range of machines from small MacPlusses to MacIIs with A3 or A4 screens, some of them colour. 'Not every job requires a big screen. We would like to give everyone a large screen, but it's not a priority.' At the heart of the system lie the Linotronic typesetting machines, connected to the computers through a device rather ominously called an RIP (it actually stands for Raster Image Processor). Although laser printers are used for proofing, only the 1200 dpi or even 2500 dpi resolution of the Linotronics will satisfy the demands of graphic design professionals.

Typesetting through this sort of setup can still be a difficult business. Graphics particularly are prone to come out in the wrong place, or with lines too thick or too thin. Patrick is proud of his 'Mr Fix-it' image, and will happily work on into the evening to get a job right. 'Solving a problem no one else has been able to solve' is his biggest reward.

Working with the general public also brings extra headaches. He needs to keep up with every development of every program that might conceivably be used to typeset from. Some produce excellent output; some cause problems. He stresses to customers that it is as important to know the limitations of their machines as it is to know the capabilities. Sometimes pasting a graphic in by hand can be better in every respect than trying to re-create it on screen.

CHAPTER 8

USING THE TECHNOLOGY

This chapter is about desktop publishing (DTP). In theory, DTP means publishing with just the equipment that will fit on your desk. In practise, it means any sort of personal publishing using the new, computer-based publishing technology.

If you choose to publish using DTP, you are joining a revolution. Five years ago the equipment around which most of this book is based did not exist. Now, the equipment exists and our skills and attitudes need to change to keep pace.

New technology has made several major changes in the way we work. It allows us to alter text easily and quickly, to merge text and graphics without the problems of pasting up and to print out at a superbly high degree of resolution.

Most of all, it allows the author of a document to take control over the way that it is produced. This 'democratisation of print' is one of the major driving forces behind the DTP revolution.

You might think that, with such benefits, DTP would be irresistible. Yet some people do fight shy of it, and for very good reasons. Before you choose, therefore, whether to join the revolution, review these advantages and limitations .

Advantages
- Compared to traditional professional methods (ie, typesetting and pasting up), the new technology is quicker, cheaper and gives you more control.
- Compared with traditional amateur publishing methods (ie, typing on a typewriter, pasting up, photocopying), the new technology is quicker, makes an upmarket look easily accessible, is less messy and demands and gives a feeling of professionalism.
- Some things, such as distorted text and wrap-arounds, are possible using DTP that are either not possible any other way or would otherwise be so expensive as to be impractical.

Limitations
- DTP involves a high capital cost, requires computer skills and can limit creativity and flair.
- The formal look of laser-printed documents can put some people off: documents that were fun to produce and read can be spoiled by an obsession with quality of print.
- Conversely, DTP is still sneered at by some professional designers and typesetters.

What are the basics?

There are many elements to a DTP system, but very few of them are essential. In fact, any computer with a printer will be able to get you into print.

That said, some systems will allow you to use the new technology properly, whereas with others you will still essentially be using traditional publishing methods.

On this page, as a starting point for understanding and choosing a DTP system, we outline the basic building blocks of a comprehensive system. The system is illustrated overleaf. It may be what you will aim for, in time, if you are using DTP professionally. Occasional users and those with low budgets can get away with much less.

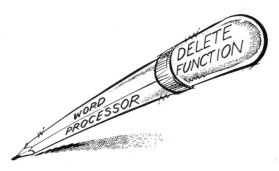

- Computer: this, the central and controlling element of the system, is the box containing the actual electronics. Some computers need additional circuit boards (called expansion cards) to handle top-quality screens or printers.
- Screen: there are three important things to consider - size, shape and resolution. The screen resolution dictates how much detail and clarity you get, and depends on the number of dots per square inch (dpi).
- Mouse: this is the essential tool for DTP because it allows you to move text and images around on the screen.
- Keyboard: any keyboard will do, as the mouse will do most of the command work.
- Software: programs that let computers carry out your instructions. The right software may be the starting point when you choose your system.

- Floppy discs: these store and transfer information. The disc itself is contained in a stiff plastic envelope. All computers use them; smaller ones use only floppies for storage.
- Hard discs: a hard disc, like a floppy disc, stores information, but much more of it. You will always need floppies, if only to load programs into the hard disc initially, but a hard disc can save you the time and temper of constantly having to switch floppies when changing programs. The extra space on a hard disc is useful for DTP, which tends to demand a great deal of information storage. A hard disc can be built into the computer, or be separate, as in our illustration.
- Printer: there are several printer options. We have illustrated a laser printer, the machine that sparked off the DTP revolution.
- Scanner: a scanner allows you to transform drawings or photographs into a form that the computer can understand, show on screen and print out. They are essential for some applications, although, for much DTP, traditional paste-up works just as well.

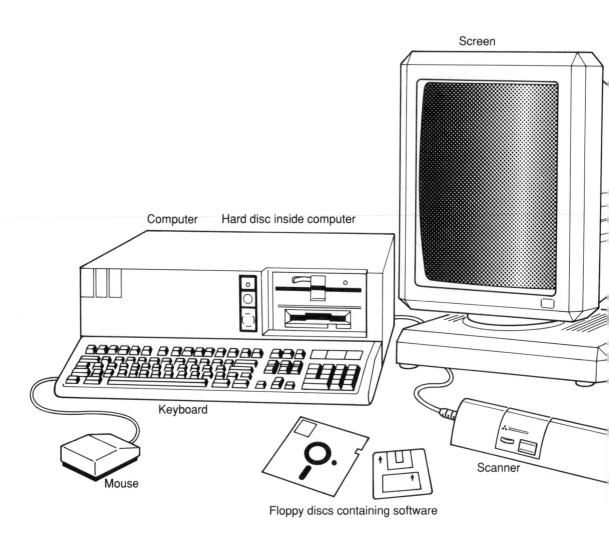

Screen

Computer   Hard disc inside computer

Keyboard

Mouse

Floppy discs containing software

Scanner

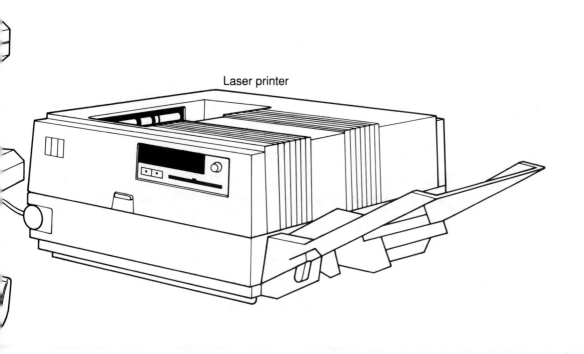

Laser printer

Picking the appropriate technology

What system will you choose? How will you decide? We first offer some background information about how systems have developed and how this affects DTP. Then we suggest criteria to use when choosing, and ways to get support for the process.

Menus and commands

Despite the fact that the electronic computer is as old an invention as the jet aeroplane, many people see them as mysterious devices, at best incomprehensible, at worst positively malign.

Computer manufacturers have long sought to make computers 'friendly' to use. The first problem was that a computer was operated by typing in a series of seemingly illogical directions or 'commands' such as 'F1' or 'Option S'. Mentally linking keyboard strokes such as these with natural instructions such as 'Make this bold' or 'Move this section to there' was not only a difficult feat of memory, but also made using a computer an unfamiliar and unintuitive task.

The first attempt to make the computer friendlier was to present a restaurant-type menu of numbered options on the screen. To choose a function, you simply typed the appropriate number. This approach, though, proved unwieldy and time-consuming.

Obviously a completely different approach was required if computers and people were ever going to get along together. By the 1970s, research teams all over the world were working on the problem. The winning solution was the WIMP interface described

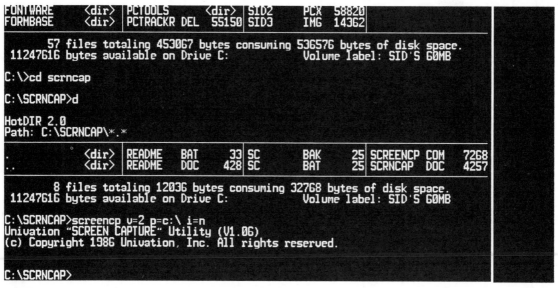

Non-WIMP screen showing file directories

overleaf and developed originally by Xerox Corporation.

In one of the great coups of commercial history, the entire research team was persuaded to defect to Apple, where what they had learned was put to use in creating a computer called the Lisa, which subsequently became the Macintosh. Other WIMP machines followed, as did two add-on systems for the IBM PC: Windows and GEM. Finally, however, in 1989 even IBM capitulated and produced a new range of computers using a WIMP system called Presentation Manager.

Unfortunately, this does not mean that you can now buy any computer confident that it will have a WIMP system. Presentation Manager only works on IBM's larger personal computers. Other machines tend to have hybrid systems with elements of both types of

system – WIMP and typed commands.

Nearly all DTP software demands WIMP, so it is common to buy a machine that has a mouse but only use it while running the DTP program. While using other programs such as word processors, or doing housekeeping tasks such as copying files between discs, you are back to typed commands.

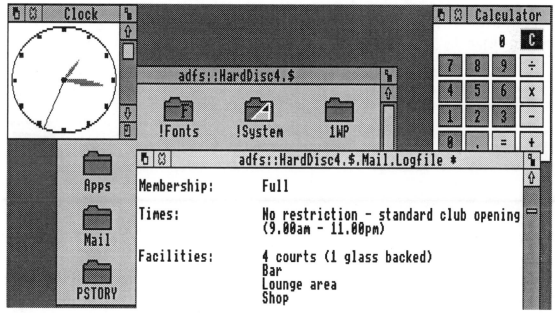

WIMP screen with four open windows containing clock, file directory, text and calculator

How WIMPs work

WIMP stands for Windows, Icons, Menus and Pointers. The system is most readily decribed by working backwards through the acronym.

A Pointer is a visual device, such as an arrow, that can be used to point at different items, such as words or graphic objects, on the screen. You move the pointer around using the mouse described on page 101. One of the types of object you will point at is a Menu.

This is different from the menus used in earlier systems, in that they 'pop up' or 'pull down'. The menu heading is permanently visible at the top or bottom of the screen. You point at this and click the button on your mouse to make the rest of the menu appear. Similarly, you select items from the menu by clicking on them rather than by typing a number.

You might also point and click on an Icon. This is a symbol representing a file or a function; it works on the same principle as having a figure of a man or woman on a toilet door. Clicking on a program icon will instruct the computer to run that program. Within the program you might also find icons representing tools; a pencil, for example,

might indicate to the computer that you want to draw a line - something you would then do with the mouse, of course.

A Window is an area of the computer's screen in which you can see your work in progress, as if looking through a window in a building. You might have more than one window open on the screen at once.

What to consider

We now move to considering how to make your choice of system. We have identified 16 different issues to consider.

- Does (or can) your system use WIMPs?
- What is the printer quality? Does the printer use PostScript? PostScript is a new technique, described on page 152, that allows complex typesetting. In general, if you want text presentation of anything approaching typeset quality, you will need PostScript.
- Is it a colour or monochrome system? Colour is expensive and not needed in normal DTP work, but may be necessary for other ways that you intend to use the computer.
- How big is the system's memory? Memory is measured in *bytes*. A kilobyte (K) is 1024 bytes, a megabyte (M) is 1024 kilobytes. A byte consists of 8 bits, the fundamental units of information.
- What other features are available on the system? Some machines that offer good publishing software also offer games, accounts packages, databases, outliners.
- What software is available? You may well want to identify the software you want before choosing your hardware.

- If you are only buying one element of a system, is it compatible with other equipment already bought? Equally, if you are buying the basics, make sure you can add what you want later.
- Is the system you are considering compatible with systems owned by people with whom you are working? Check the machines in your working environment, and also what systems are used by people who may be able to give you support.
- What formal and informal support is available? See our notes on page 163. Remember that getting full training can cost you as much as your hardware did.
- Is the system you are considering new and therefore having teething troubles?
- Equally, is the system 'future-proofed'? A computer based on old technology won't run up-to-date software.
- Is your system easy to work with? If you are using your system every day, you will want to be sure that it is. Consider screen resolution, colour and size. A resolution of 70 dpi is minimal; there should be no flicker; monochrome screens are more restful; and the larger the screen, the better.
- What sort of training time does it involve for you and any potential users?
- What is the cost? Consider not only the short-term expenditure to buy the basics, but also the long-term cost when you want to expand your system.
- What is the system's image? Some have a business image, others an amateur or cult image.

- What does the system look like? If your office is in a family room, this is a vital issue!

In general, we found that, once people have made the decision and bought a system, they do feel they have made the right choice. In fact, people become 'pair-bonded' to the system they buy, and thereafter defend it fiercely!

Who can help?

Most people begin by gathering information on paper. This might be through magazines or buyers' guides, although many of them are aimed at the already converted. Publicity material and seminars from dealers and makers are also a good, if biased, source.

When you are ready to try out the one or two systems that you think you might want, you will need to get 'hands on' experience. We found, and our sentiments were unfortunately echoed all too often by people we talked to, that dealers often fail to find out the needs of the customer before giving demonstrations or making recommendations.

Friends will take things more slowly and may give you time to 'play' on their machines. Keep in mind what you need from a system; your friends' needs may be different. If none of your friends have systems, try contacting a user group and asking if any of its members would let you have an evening's hands-on experience. Then, if you choose to buy that system, you have friendly support from the start.

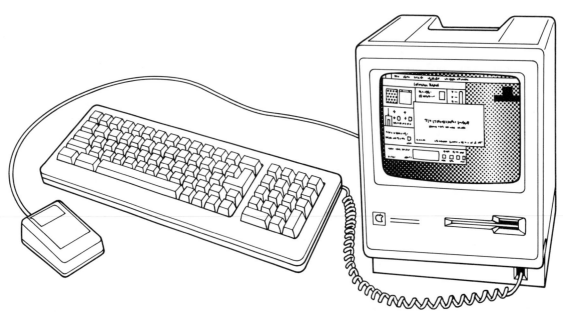

Apple Macintosh

The 'Mac', as it is universally known, was one of the first computers to offer an exclusively WIMP environment, and it is still the easiest computer to use. It was originally designed to be a 'productivity tool' that anyone could use without knowing anything about programs or programming. Since it was launched, the Mac has attracted an intensely loyal following; probably in response to feeling isolated in the sea of far more numerous IBM clones, Mac people tend to club together, and won't hear a word spoken against their beloved machines.

It is the computer on which DTP started, and perhaps because of this has become the almost universal machine for DTP and graphics professionals. It is worth remembering, however, that the Mac was invented before DTP, and has as many

non-DTP uses as any other computer. It is increasingly being taken up by large and small businesses alike for all kinds of computing tasks. If you really want to get an idea of its range, try to get hold of a few copies of the excellent (and free!) magazine *Apple Business*, which regularly reviews interesting applications in all fields.

The minute you switch on a Mac, you can see that it was designed to sit on your desk, switched on all day, every day. The screen looks enough like a piece of paper that it does not shock the eye or demand attention. A typical session involves using not only the program you are working in, but also the 'desk accessories', extra programs such as a calculator, an address file or the Scrapbook mentioned on page 126, which can be used at the same time as the work you are doing.

DTP on the Mac does have one frustration; with the standard, small screen, working on an A4 page is like using a magnifying glass to read - although the image is very clear, you can only see part of it at a time. You have to steer yourself round the page by using the mouse.

In common with all computers, the Mac has been developed and expanded as processing power and, more importantly, memory becomes cheaper and more available. When it first came out it had 128 kilobytes (conventionally shortened to 128K) of memory. Although 128K was a lot by the standards of the day, it was not really enough to power the WIMP system, so the 512K 'Fat Mac' was introduced. This was shortly followed by the MacPlus with one megabyte.

This is now the standard 'small' Mac. The range stretches from that to several variants of the MacII, a massively powerful machine with up to 5M of memory, and capable of running several colour screens at once. Apple's range of products also includes its own range of laser printers, which, while expensive, have the advantage of working the minute you plug them in - a rarity in the computer industry.

Macs won't run IBM compatible software, and can only read files created by conventional word processors, for example, with extreme difficulty and much faffing about. This is important if you already work alongside PCs and have a real need for compatibility. There are exceptions to this; Word 4.0 and PageMaker 3.0 are available in versions for both machines, and can share files; some organisations, such as the Open University, operate a dual-platform principle whereby they accept material on Mac and IBM formats.

The price for all this power and convenience is high; the Mac is a very expensive computer to own, although prices at the bottom end of the range are coming down.

Pro
- It is the easiest machine to set up, to learn and to use.
- Information can be moved easily between different kinds of program.
- The best DTP software is available first or only on the Mac.
- There is a supportive Mac community.
- It has a high-resolution screen.
- PostScript printer support is (almost) standard.

Con
- There is no cheap way into owning Macs. The set-up cost is considerably more expensive than for a comparably powerful PC, unless you include training costs in your calculations.
- Except for the more expensive machines in the range, Macs come with small screens.
- If you are already trained to use a command-line based system, the WIMP interface will feel frustratingly slow for some tasks.
- No IBM compatibility, except on the MacII, or via a network that connects different machines together.

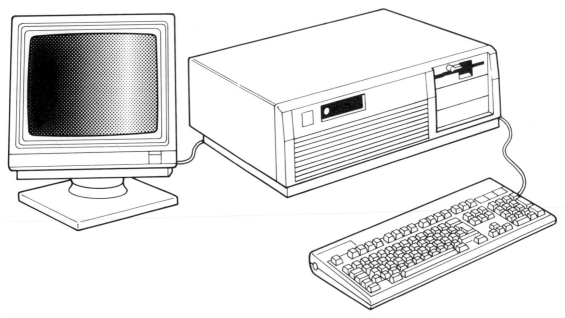

IBM PC

PC is a generic label for an IBM Personal Computer or any of the hundreds of copies on the market. Despite the claims of other manufacturers, it is still *the* business microcomputer. The original machine was designed for word processing and accounting programs, and had a minimum of frills. Once you had learned your program you stuck to it, and it served well as an admin tool.

As the computer market has grown, the PC has grown with it. With each new need, an extension has been developed to meet it. So PCs now come with fast processors, colour screens, hard discs and any kind of printer you like. These developments have, however, been produced piecemeal, and have thus created a confusing plethora of different standards so that you can no longer assume

that any one piece of equipment will work with another, or with a particular program.

Similarly, the huge number of machines in use has created a viable market for specialist software. So, for example, a market gardener somewhere in the world has probably already created a scheduling package that will help you to plan your companion planting to get a maximum yield for a given climate, soil type and so on. The problem, of course, is that it can be very difficult to find out that this program even exists, let alone get hold of a copy.

The unfortunate thing about the PC is that its success is due less to technical merit than to IBM's commercial dominance of the computer market. This has led to something of a psychological block on the part of buyers, who have tended to put 'IBM compatibility' at the top of their criteria list, whether or not it is something they really need.

In fact, the PC suffers two important limitations that its rivals do not. Firstly, it is designed as a non-WIMP, text-based machine. The WIMP systems that are now available for it, such as Microsoft Windows, are rather uncomfortable add-ons that cannot run all the programs available for the machine. Secondly, its memory is limited to only 640K by its design. When the PC was designed, this seemed like a massive amount; now, compared with 4M in the relatively low-cost Atari ST or Acorn Archimedes, 640K looks a little silly. Memory expansion is now possible, but it requires extra trouble and expense, and not all programs can use it once you have got it installed.

The experience of using a PC for DTP varies tremendously according to what sort of machine you have and what you are using it for. Small-scale users typically aim for a middle-range 'AT' machine, adding a high-resolution screen and mouse. Smaller machines in the 'XT' range can be used for DTP but they are desperately slow and limited. They use WIMP software, either PageMaker or Ventura, but need to know enough typed-in commands to do normal computer-housekeeping tasks such as copying, moving or deleting files. They may also use other programs that use menus, but not the mouse. Essentially, the AT is two computers rolled into one; the friendly but occasionally slow WIMP machine, and the speedy 'bare bones' text-only machine. Few people like both, however, so the result can be a frustrating compromise. We recommend that if you have a PC you invest in Windows

right from the start so as to obviate the need to learn any command-line instructions.

Added to the compatibility issue, there are however some recent developments that could still make the PC a good investment. The first is PS/2, IBM's cryptic name for a new range of WIMP machines that nevertheless follows the same principles as older PCs and can run modified versions of most PC software. The other is that PC developers have been quicker off the mark than most to develop cheap alternatives to PostScript. This means that the investment needed to get top-quality graphics from your computer will only be hundreds, rather than thousands of pounds over and above the cost of the computer.

Pro
- A vast range of software. Someone, somewhere, has already come across your specialist need and written a PC program to meet it.
- Starter machines are cheap and easily available.
- Most businesses have PCs.
- Incredible range of add-ons and add-ins.

Con
- Even if you buy Windows, you will at some stage be faced with the need to learn command line instructions.
- Making all the different bits work together is at best problematic and at worst extremely frustrating.
- Good screens, while available, put you right back into the Mac price range.
- DTP and graphics programs lag behind their Mac counterparts.

Atari ST

When the Atari ST was launched it was
promoted as a low-cost alternative to the
Macintosh. It had a WIMP system called
GEM, which is also available as an extra on
the PC. It had a powerful processor and, by
contemporary standards, plenty of memory.
What it didn't have was credibility. Atari was
known only as a manufacturer of TV games,
and had in any case changed hands shortly
before the ST launch. Inevitably, the computer
has come to be seen as 'just a games machine',
and most of its users are still hobbyists.
However, it has a lot of potential for DTP.

The ST comes in two basic forms. Smaller
ones combine the computer and keyboard
while the larger 'Mega ST' machines follow
the 'three box' format of computer, screen and
keyboard. For DTP purposes you need at least

the small-format ST1040, which has one
megabyte of memory. If you want to use a
laser printer, you need the larger Mega 2 ST or
Mega 4 ST machines, which have memories of
2M and 4M respectively.

The laser printer is one of the Atari's
major plusses. As we explain on page 152,
cheaper laser printers normally force you to
compromise between operating speed and
versatility. Even expensive PostScript ones can
take their time with complex pages.

Atari have managed to break this rule
without indulging in the expense of PostScript
by using a system called Direct Memory
Access. As the name suggests, this is a system
that zips information from the computer's
memory direct to the printer with minimal
interference. The secret is that the computer
creates an electronic picture of the page - all

eight million dots of it - in its memory before sending them to the printer. Since each dot requires one bit of memory, and there are 8 bits to a byte, this requires one megabyte of extra memory, over and above that required by the program. Hence the need for at least 2M altogether.

The upshot of all this is that the printer is much faster than any other we have seen. Its only real drawback is that it can only be connected to a single computer.

The other big plus is the screen; the ST is the only machine other than the Mac that comes with a high-resolution monochrome screen as standard. What is more, the screen is 12 inches across the diagonal compared with the Mac's 9 inches. This gives it more than half as much area again - a real improvement. There is also a low-resolution colour version, but we would advise against this.

The ST scores particularly highly in the budget DTP department. A cheap ST1040 connected to a 24-pin dot-matrix printer will produce output almost as good as the laser printer's, at least for text. The only cheaper alternative to this is the Amstrad PCW which is a much more limited machine.

Getting output that is better than laser quality is a problem. Few typesetters are able to set documents created on an Atari. However, once there are enough Atari users to make this facility commercially worthwhile, the situation will improve.

Although the range of software available for the Atari is less than that for the PC or the Mac, what there is is good - and some of it, such as the multi-lingual word processor Signum 2, is unique.

One exciting possibility is that an ST can be used as a Mac clone, in the same way as there are dozens of PC clones around. The two machines are driven by the same make and model of processor, so theoretically there is no problem. There are gadgets that are claimed to do just this; however, they need to use some secondhand parts rescued from genuine Macintoshes because Apple will not allow Atari to make their own. If you really want a Mac but cannot afford it, this might be one route to try.

Although it has been around for several years, the ST has only just burst through into being a machine that the personal publisher should take seriously. It is a particularly good option for someone who wants to set up a system on a limited budget, but has no great need for compatibility with other systems.

Pro
- WIMP interface with only a few lapses into command lines.
- Low-cost but high-quality DTP setup is possible.
- Increasing quantities of good, professional software.
- Good, cheap printers.

Con
- Not compatible with anything else.
- Amateur image.
- Low-cost, fragile construction.
- Cheaper models are just games machines.
- Typesetting resources scarce.
- Few DTP users, so little likelihood of community support.

Amstrad PCW

PCW stands for Personal Computer Wordprocessor. The PCW is designed first and foremost as an alternative to the typewriter. It is used by authors, journalists and community groups.

The PCW comes in two versions, one with a dot-matrix printer, the other with a daisywheel printer. If you are planning to use one to produce your document directly, we recommend that you buy the daisywheel option because of its greatly superior readability. Using the PCW involves learning either the menu-driven LocoScript program, which comes with the computer, or one of the command-driven word processors that are available (we recommend the excellent New Word). Producing your flier or newsletter will then involve one of two options: taking a disc to a laser or typesetting bureau that can convert it (like the Neal's Yard bureau featured on page 151), or manually pasting up your output with any illustrations.

Pro
- Incredibly cheap.
- Uses existing business software, including databases, spreadsheets etc.
- Community support.
- Can be used for typesetting.

Con
- Hard to learn.
- Low-resolution screen creates eye fatigue.
- No page makeup or graphics software that we could recommend.
- Not WYSIWYG, so typesetting must be calculated carefully.

Commodore Amiga

The history of computing is littered with great leaps forward that somehow never landed again, and the Amiga is a classic example of this syndrome.

It was originally designed as a business machine that would completely outperform all others; not only did it have a colour WIMP system, but it also offered multi-tasking. This is a really useful facility that allows the user to run more than one program at once, moving between them at will. So you can write your great novel at the same time as calculating the pools odds, or work on the company report and check the accounts database at the same time. The Mac and the PC are only just now catching up with multi-tasking.

Nevertheless, the Amiga too fell into the 'games machine' trap, probably because of its other strong point – animation. This has, however, led to a major commercial application now being called Desk Top Video (DTV). Training, demonstration and promotion tapes can be edited or created using the machine at a fraction of the cost of conventional techniques. While this is a form of publishing in its own right, we were able to find very little support for DTP on the Amiga.

Pro
- Could move you into getting your message across via the very powerful medium of video.

Con
- As a DTP machine it loses out to others on ability, cost and compatibility.

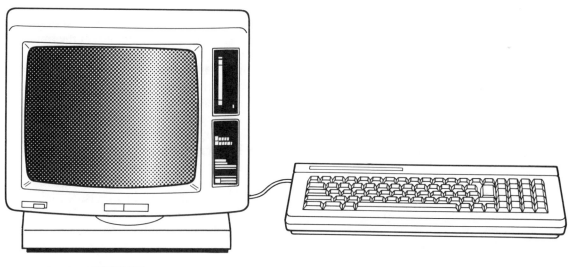

Amstrad PCW8256

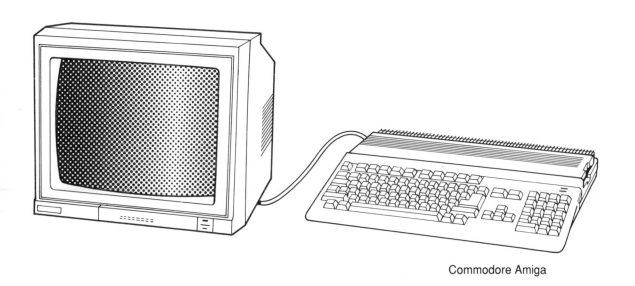

Commodore Amiga

Acorn Archimedes

The Acorn Archimedes is the first Reduced Instruction Set Computer (RISC). This technical acronym means that it works much faster than any other microcomputer of similar size. It has a very neat WIMP system; where other computers have to use up precious screen space on the menu bar, an area to which you point to call up a menu, the Archimedes uses the mouse to create a 'menu of menus' anywhere on the screen.

The problem with the Archimedes is a 'Catch 22' one. Because the DTP software available for it does not match up to the competition, few people will buy an Archimedes for DTP purposes. Similarly, because few people use the Archimedes for DTP, few publishers will invest in writing software for it.

It is likely to become particularly popular in the education market. Acorn make the BBC Micro which, while long in the tooth, is used and loved by schools all over the country. These same schools will probably upgrade to the Archimedes, thus ensuring a good market for, and ready supply of, educational software.

Pro
- Super-fast RISC processor.
- Full specification for its price.
- Good support in and for education.
- Clever multi-tasking WIMP system.

Con
- Another fresh start means little compatibility with other machines.
- No good DTP software, and no prospect of catching up with other machines.

NeXT

The NeXT is the most recently launched of the computers we review here; in fact, at the time of writing, none have yet reached the UK. It was launched by former Apple boss Steve Jobs as something that would be a quantum leap beyond Apple's Macintosh. Its standard features are expensive options on other machines: a large, very high-resolution screen, Display PostScript, a laser printer and disc drives that can hold almost a *thousand* times as much information as conventional floppies.

The thing that really distinguishes the NeXT from other machines reviewed here is that behind the WIMP interface lurks an operating system called Unix, which has been used on large computers for years. This gives the NeXT instant compatibility with thousands of specialised business, engineering and academic programs, including the powerful (and expensive) document processor, Interleaf.

NeXT will probably sell well, since it only costs the same as a small car. However, it will be several years before there are good DTP programs for it that really use its power.

Pro
- Big enough to run a corporation, or two.
- Industry standard Unix system means that lots of high-powered programs only need modifying to run.
- Incredibly cheap for its power.
- Fashionable image.

Con
- A sledgehammer to crack the DTP nut.
- Not proven.

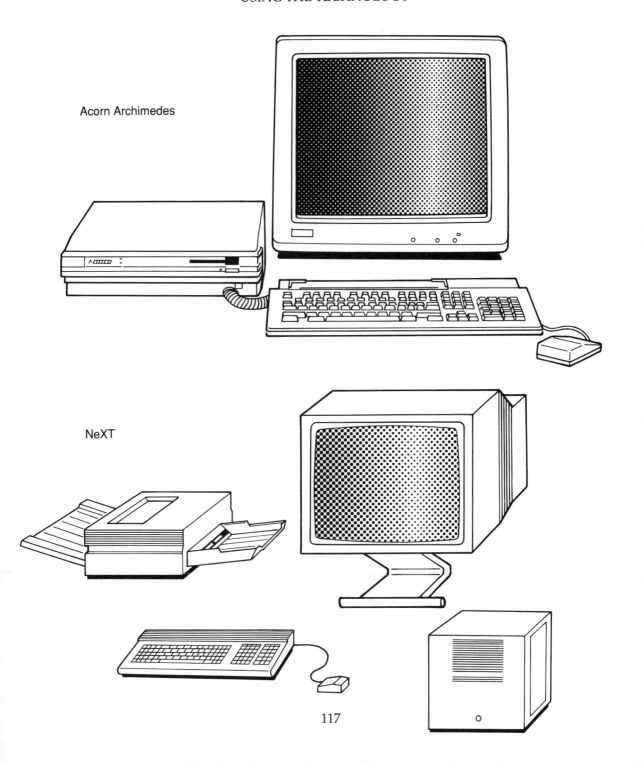

Acorn Archimedes

NeXT

WHRRIC

The Women's Health and Reproductive Rights Information Centre (WHRRIC) is a women's collective that gives health information and support. They're spread through several floors of a modern block near the City of London, and combine a whole host of activities, including a phone enquiry service, an extensive library, contact with local support groups as well as producing health fact sheets, publicity leaflets and a regular newsletter.

Three years ago, the whole collective turned their publishing activities over to DTP. At first it was fairly hard. 'We knew nothing. We had help from Microsyster, the women's computer consultancy, and there was someone in the building who knew about computers; you need somebody on hand when you're learning'. Three years later, they now feel they are 'computer comfortable'.

Their system consists of three Zeniths with laser printer. They type in copy, usually written in-house or by commissioned writers, using WordStar. Then they transfer the text to Ventura Publisher using a style sheet they've developed. At first they made the classic beginners' mistake, using 'every font we could find ... now we use very few!'

Illustrations slot into gaps left in the copy. They get some from other magazines, some they commission and 'if we review a book, we usually get our printer to screen in a reduced photograph of the front cover'. Laser copy and all the other elements are pasted up at WHRRIC, and the printer, with whom they work 'very closely indeed', takes it from there.

One of the really impressive things about WHRRIC is that they use the new technology in a number of supporting roles. Their database of health contacts and index to library resources are on computer, as is the mailing list for the newsletter.

The crunch comes when there is 'competition for the computers', but they reckon the benefits are worth it. 'We save money, we cut out huge stages from the process, we keep control. And, it's fun!'

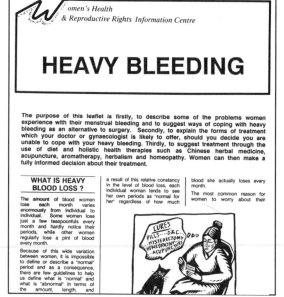

Software - layout packages

Even years ago, what appeared on a computer screen was not what would be output from a printer. There were no on-screen representations of typefaces, weights, sizes of letters, graphics or layout. It was impossible to make judgements or decisions about these things, or manipulate layout elements on screen to get the right effect. Nowadays we have WYSIWYG (What You See Is What You Get), which gives us all the above things, and so makes DTP an accessible reality.

WYSIWYG requires two things: a high-resolution screen (see pages 159-60) and appropriate software. At the moment, this combination is only available on the PC, the Mac and the ST. On other machines you are better off using either straight word processing or an encoding system such as those mentioned in our profiles of *Ram News* (page 57) and Neal's Yard DTP Studio (page 151).

Assuming that you do want to use layout software, it is worth taking the time to understand some of the principles on which it is based. This will give you the essential tools to appraise for yourself programs that we have not reviewed in this book, either because of lack of space or because they had not been published at the time of writing.

Layout software can be categorised in two ways. Is it page- or document-oriented? Is it column- or grid-based? You should note, however, that the leading packages tend to cross these boundaries as their publishers try to grab their competitors' markets by copying features of their programs.

Page- or document-oriented?

Page-oriented software has the main unit of work as the page. An example is Calamus, described in more detail on page 140.

Each page of a document is treated as a separate entity and doesn't flow on to the next. Hence it requires a specific operation to change from one page to the next, and edits involving the whole document - such as correcting a misspelt name throughout - take a great deal of time and energy.

Conversely, such packages allow a lot more flexibility in creating individual page designs. Use them for documents where each page has a different layout, such as news sheets.

Document-oriented software has the main unit of work as the document. Ventura Publisher, covered in more detail on page 139, is the classic example. Some of the more powerful word processors can also fairly claim to be document processors.

The document-oriented package sets up a template with parameters that apply to the whole document. Each page is the same, and flows on one from another.

Once you have typed your text, using a separate word processing package, you drop it into a template. The text then flows happily on through the document; the program creates page breaks where necessary, and forms as many pages as are appropriate. If you need to change something, a few commands will alter it throughout the document, a facility that is excellent for ensuring consistency.

These packages are ideal for documents where every page is the same, such as novels. They make consistency (and thus editing)

 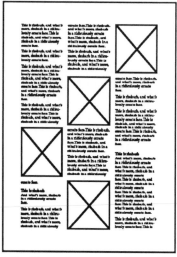 

A three-page grid-oriented document; the illustrations are indicated by crossed boxes. The document grid has three vertical and four horizontal divisions, and each element (title, text, illustrations) takes up one or more square of the grid.

very easy, and take a lot of the decisions out of your hands. If you want variable page layout, for a magazine or brochure, document-oriented packages work far less well.

Column- or grid-oriented?

Broadly speaking, there are two approaches to laying out a page: columns or grids. Designers of books and manuals tend to think in terms of layouts of one, two or three columns, sometimes broken to allow space for an illustration. The production of magazines, advertising literature and complex written material, however, requires an approach in which different elements, whether text or graphics, are each assigned a space on a grid which divides the page into rectangles.

All page/document makeup software follows one or the other of these two principles. Text is inserted into the pages in text 'boxes' and the position of these boxes is determined by the underlying column or gid format. The better packages of either kind are capable of producing good quality output suitable for both books and magazines, so it is best to decide between the two according to which approach feels most natural to you.

Column-based packages are currently far more common in the UK than are grid-based ones. In part this is because the two best known DTP packages for the PC, Xerox Ventura Publisher and Aldus PageMaker, are both primarily column-based.

Their main advantage is that text flows from the bottom of one column to the top of the next, from left to right across the page. This means that, when you import a big chunk

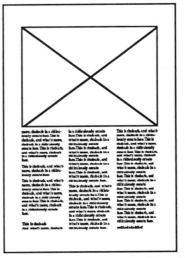
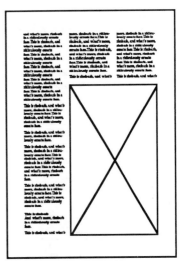

A three-page column-oriented document; the illustrations are indicated by crossed boxes. The columns are not divided horizontally and each element may take up any portion of a column.

of text, it will all go where you expect it to. Through the use of movable vertical guides it is also partcularly easy to create columns of irregular widths. Where illustrations are inserted, the text simply jumps past them, allowing them to be placed in the middle of columns without interrupting the flow.

Many word processors now offer multi-column formats and the ability to draw in illustrations, so the distinction between these and column-based page makeup packages has blurred. If your document is, for example, a self-published novel, it could be that a good word processor will serve your needs better.

Grid-based packages are modelled on traditional manual paste-up methods, which start with a grid of fine lines that mark out a set of rectangles on to a baseboard. Different elements of the page are then pasted into the rectangles, but every baseboard is the same; this imposes a sense of order on to the whole document. This book, for example, is created on a grid two boxes wide and four deep. Although text does not always start at the top of the page, if you leaf through the book you will notice that text always starts in one of four positions, corresponding to the top of a box.

In a grid-based layout package, the grid is the first thing to be set up. Boxes for text and graphics are then drawn on to the page and tucked snugly up against the gridlines. Finally, text and graphics are entered in the boxes.

Since there is no hard-and-fast rule as to how text should flow from box to box on the page, an essential tool is the 'linker'. As its

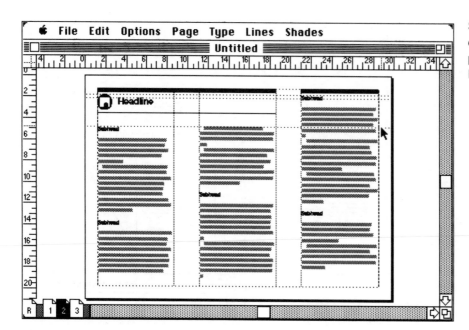

Screen dump of column-based package (Aldus PageMaker)

name implies, this allows you to show the program where to place continued text that is too long for one box.

Grid-based programs will do particularly well if the kind of documents you want to produce do not fall into a standard format, or if you are a graphic artist who is planning to move across to computer-based production.

Choosing your software
As we mentioned towards the start of this chapter, if you are planning to buy a DTP system the first choice you make could be your software, with the hardware that runs it being of secondary importance. The choice is an important one; our research shows that most people remain loyal to the program they first learn. If you can develop that loyalty towards the one that meets your needs most

efficiently, you will clearly benefit. These are some of the questions that you might bear in mind when choosing.

- Are you trying to design pages or automate your document production?
- How complex are the layouts you want to produce?
- Do you need colour separation facility?
- What do the people around you use?
- Is the program new and buggy or mature and solid?
- When you see it, does it live up to its hype?
- How much does it cost to buy?
- How much time and money will it cost you (and your team/staff) to learn?
- If you are looking for people to work with or for you, is the program one that many people are trained on?

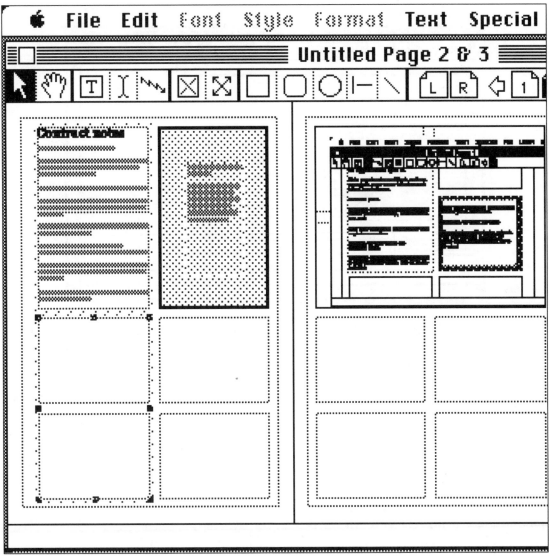

Screen dump of grid-based package (Ready,Set,Go!)

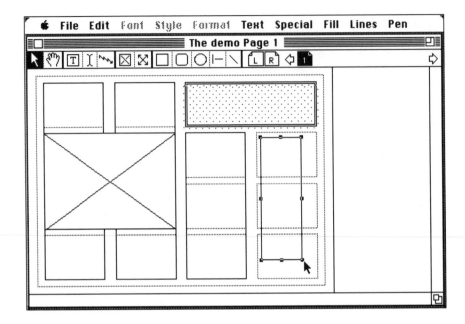

How to achieve page makeup

In order to show you the kind of general approach needed for page layout, this next section goes through, step by step, the page makeup of a small (and entirely fictional!) newsletter.

All the pictures in this section are 'screen dumps', pictures of the computer screen as we see it. The program used is Ready,Set,Go! 4.5.

Notice the screen setup in the picture above. Along the top is the Ready,Set,Go! menu bar, while below it is a row of icons representing the different tools that will be used in the page makeup process. The shaded bars on the right-hand side and bottom of the window are scroll bars which allow us to move our view of the document from side to side and up to down.

Our first step is to lay out the template for each page. The newsletter is to be printed on A4 paper, folded to make A5. We are concentrating here only on the front and back pages, which fall together on one A4 spread.

We have set up a template of four boxes horizontally, and four vertically. We've then used the grid as a guide to create four columns capable of holding text. You can see that the final column on the right-hand side is just being set up, inserted by the arrow tool. The setup of the grid allows 0.5 mm gutters between columns.

On the right-hand page, we have pulled out a box for the newsletter masthead (title), filled it with a light, 10 per cent tint, and placed a rule around it. On the left-hand page, we have pulled out a box for a picture, indicated by the crossed rectangle.

Creating the masthead

The next stage is to drop in a masthead for the newsletter. Here, we have zoomed in to show the right-hand page at full size. The text looks dotty on screen; however, the final laser output will be smooth.

To set the masthead, we have typed the text into the text box - there is only a small amount of text to be dealt with, so this is more appropriate than using a word processor and then pasting the text in.

Having typed it in, we can 'select' the text when we work with it. The dark shading over the word 'Demo' indicates that it is currently selected. Because we are working with the text, the tint and box rule we have already placed for the masthead have disappeared,

leaving us free to concentrate on the text.

For the masthead, we chose the display typeface University Roman. We set the title in 72 point, the subtitle in 18 point and the issue number in 12 point. This gives a solid feel to the main title, with the issue number a great deal smaller and less important. We emphasise this by centring the titles and ranging the issue number to the right. The shape in the centre of the letter 'D' in 'Demo' is a tool called the Ibeam, used for working with text.

For further issues of this newsletter, we would retain the layout style of two columns per page, and also the masthead style. We would change only the issue number and body text.

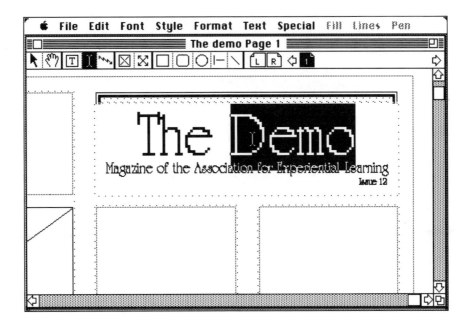

Importing the illustration

Before 'importing' or bringing in the main body of the text, we bring in the illustration. This lets us know just how much space we have left for text, so we can cut it accordingly if there are any problems.

Unlike the masthead, the illustration has been created and stored elsewhere on the system, in a program file called Scrapbook. We have used this illustration for other things, and will continue to keep it available for further use.

The first step is to indicate to the program the space on the left-hand page where the illustration is to go; as a result, the illustration space takes on a 'jigsaw' effect, that you can see on the left-hand side of the screen. Then we fetch the illustration we want from the Scrapbook file, and this appears on screen, in a window over the main newsletter file.

Getting a copy of the picture in the Scrapbook on to the selected area of the newsletter is a two-stage process. The picture is first copied into an intermediate file called the Clipboard, using the Copy command from the Edit menu.

We can then close the Scrapbook and, using the next command down on the Edit menu, Paste the picture from the Clipboard on to the writing page.

The ability to copy and paste almost anything to or from a clipboard is one of the essential components of any DTP system.

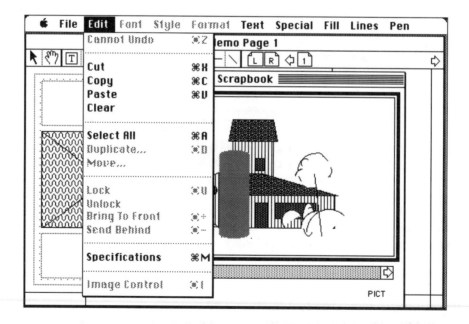

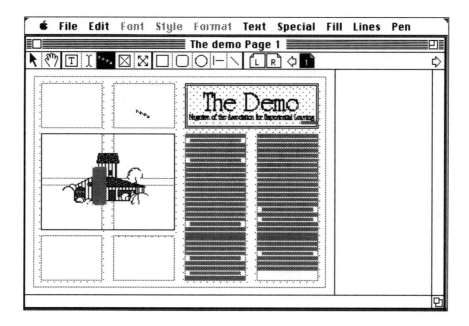

Importing the text

Unlike the masthead, the body text for this newsletter is not typed in directly to the page layout program. It has been typed in previously to a word processing program, and we import it into the newsletter in much the same way as we imported the illustration.

The text is to go in more than one column on the spread, so we have to link columns to allow the text to flow from one to another. We do this by using the linking tool, which you can see as a lightning symbol on the top right-hand column of the back page of the newsletter. You can tell that it is in use because, on the line of pointers at the top of the screen, the linker tool is highlighted.

In this picture, text has already flowed into both columns on the front page of the newsletter. As you will see later, the text will flow around the illustration on the back page; the program can handle this, to create interesting positioning of text and graphics.

The screen dump picture is very small scale, and it is totally impossible to read the text on it. However, to make it even easier on the eye, the system has 'greeked' the text, turning it into simple, straight lines that merely indicate text positioning. This is particularly useful when looking at overall layout and design of a page, and deciding where text and illustrations are best placed.

The text box on the right-hand column of the left-hand page fills only three of the boxes. This is because we are inserting a small 'details' box, separate from the main text boxes, in this space.

Setting the text

The text imported from the word processing program had no specific typographical form. We now have to create that form with instructions to the program. Having selected the block of text we are going to set (you can see it reversed out on the left-hand side of the screen), we call up the Style Specifications window to set its parameters.

While this is fairly self-explanatory, two points are worth mentioning. Firstly, the style has a name, 'Text'. Once created, we can call it by name and apply it to whatever text we like, without having to reset all the parameters. Secondly, the line spacing is set to 'Auto', meaning that we let the program work it out. In this case, the program will use a 14 point line spacing, allowing a generous 2 points of leading between the 12 point characters. This looks good on a laser printer, but is a little wide if we decide to typeset.

Bits and pieces

To complete the setting, we add a caption to the picture, and a small text box of details, both on the left-hand page.

The caption received its own text box, under the illustration, so that we could create a new style specification for it alone. We made the caption Optima Bold 24 point, centred and underlined. We tend to avoid underlining where possible, but in this case, to separate the caption from the text that flowed round it, the rule created by underlining was a good idea.

The details box was set in Optima 12 point, with the address pulled out in Optima Oblique.

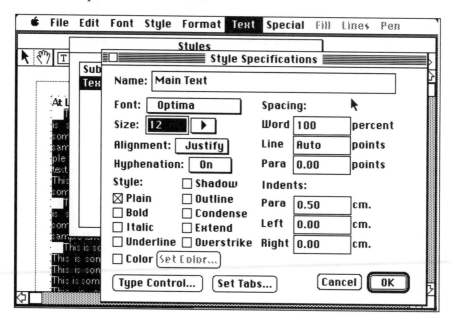

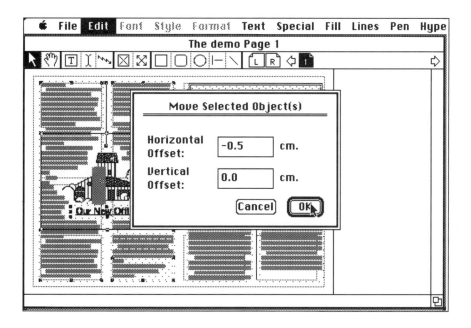

Final tidying

The newsletter, A4 to be folded to A5, was originally set, for ease, as a set of four columns equally divided with 1 cm gutters. However, we really want a large central gutter, so that, when folded, each page has an equal margin of 1 cm.

Unfortunately, unequal grid spacing is still beyond the abilities of the program, so we cheated by setting extra wide (1.5 cm) left and right margins instead.

When the setting was done, and we were ready to adjust the grid to the final position we wanted, we could have chosen to move the completed text and illustration boxes by eye to the correct position on each page. Ready,Set,Go! has, however, a facility for automatic offset. This is shown in the picture above.

We instructed a move of 0.5 cm (5 mm) horizontally and in a 'negative' direction (that is, for the left-hand text boxes, moving them to the left).

Doing this for all the objects on each page created a spread with 1 cm margins, 1 cm gutters and a 2 cm middle gutter, which, when folded, creates two 1 cm margins.

At Long Last!

This is some sample text. This is some sample text. This is some sample text. This is some sample text. This is some sample text. This is some sample text. This is some sample text. This is some sample text. This is some sample text.

This is some sample text. This is some sample text. This is some sample text.

This is some sample text. This is some sample text. This is some sample text. This is some sample text. This is some sample text.

This is some sample text. This is some sample text. This is some sample text.

Our New Office

This is some sample text. This is some sample text. This is some sample text. This is some sample text.

This is some sample text. This is some sample text. This is some sample text. This is some sample text. This is some sample text.

This is some sample text. This is some sample text. This is

some sample text. This is some sample text. This is some sample text. This is some sample text. This is some sample text. This is some sample text. This is some sample text.

More Space for Demos

This is some sample text. This is some sample text. This is some sample text. This is some sample text.

This is some sample text. This is some sample text. This is some sample text. This is some sample text. This is some sample text. This is some sample text. This is some sample text. This is some sample text. This is some sample text.

Write to *The Demo*!

Got a process point to make? Why not share it with our other readers. The address is

AEL
377 Midwinter Boulevard
Central Milton Keynes
MK9 1AA

The Demo

Magazine of the Association for Experiential Learning

Issue 12

Regional News

This is some sample text. This is some sample text. This is some sample text. This is some sample text.

This is some sample text. This is some sample text. This is some sample text. This is some sample text. This is some sample text. This is some sample text. This is some sample text. This is some sample text. This is some sample text. This is some sample text. This is some sample text. This is some sample text.

Local News

This is some sample text. This is some sample text. This is some sample text. This is some sample text. This is some sample text. This is some sample text.

This is some sample text. This is some sample text. This is some sample text.

This is some sample text. This is some sample text. This is

some sample text. This is some sample text. This is some sample text. This is some sample text.

This is some sample text. This is some sample text. This is some sample text. This is some sample text. This is some sample text. This is some sample text. This is some sample text. This is some sample text. This is some sample text.

In Town Today

This is some sample text. This is some sample text. This is some sample text. This is some sample text. This is some sample text. This is some sample text.

This is some sample text. This is some sample text. This is some sample text. This is some sample text.

The leaflet showing the front and back page – the finished product could well have several pages folded to make the leaflet. Remember that because of the way the leaflet will be folded, the back page is laid out on the left. The complete, laser-printed product looks very different from the WYSIWYG screen displays we have seen on the previous pages. Note, for example, the difference between the University Roman masthead as it appears here and its screen representation on page 125. You can also see more clearly here that on the back page, the program has been able to wrap the body text around both the picture and its caption.

Publicity leaflet

When Suzanne Fields started talking to friends about the need for support to look good, she realised that 'there was a sound idea for a business in there somewhere'.

With ten years of experience behind her as fashion buyer for a large, provincial department store, Suzanne felt she had both the expertise and the people skills to turn her idea into reality. She started *Spectrum*, a franchised consultancy offering women personal support to work out their own fashion plan.

Launching *Spectrum*, Suzanne used the expertise of Peter, a graphic designer who used to work in the same department store. He planned a range of stationery in beige and brown which gave 'an elegant but gentle feel; we're aiming at the maturer woman who will follow fashion, but not slavishly'.

The logo, also designed by Peter using LetraStudio software, aims to carry through that same elegance. He opted for a computer-generated motif that set the name of the company in Caxton Roman Book and curved it round a circular baseline. 'It looks very simple,' explained Peter, 'but it's also very flexible. We use it on letterheads, business cards, comp slips and the folders given to clients to hold their notes.'

All *Spectrum*'s work, including the logo, is stored on computer, and adapted when they run new courses or launch in new areas. All franchisees have their own stationery, typeset from the central computer with details changed as relevant. 'Starting fresh, we were able to use the new technology,' said Suzanne, 'and we do - to the hilt!'

We illustrate here the three-fold brochure that publicises the one-day *Spectrum Image Seminars*. The three-fold is an ideal design 'because we need enough space to outline to people what the day is about, yet it must fit in a normal-sized envelope for mailing'. The back page has a tear-off form for applications, 'which leaves the rest of the leaflet intact, as a reminder'.

The leaflet is printed on 120 gsm beige paper with brown ink. The main body of the text is in Times Roman, not in Caxton Roman Book, which is a 'Display' face suitable only for large point size headings which attract attention. Peter chose Times because it picked up on the 'classic' feel and, like Caxton Roman Book, is a serifed face.

Spectrum is growing fast, but Suzanne is confident that the technology will allow her to keep pace.

spectrum...

a seminar for all women
who like to look their best

24 June 1991

Brook Conference Centre

Brookfield

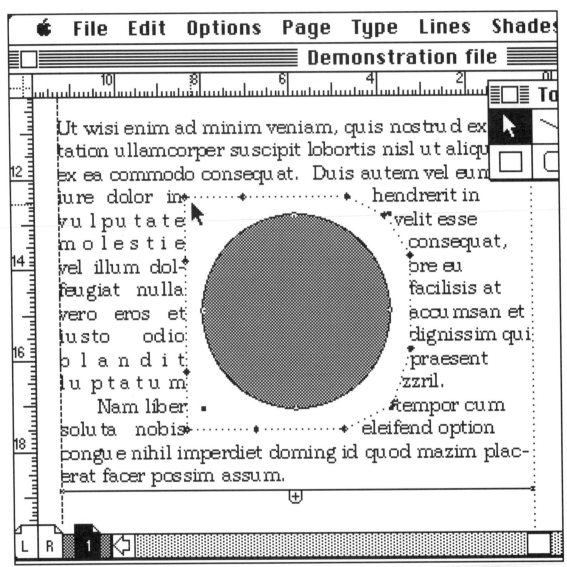

Screen dump from Aldus PageMaker. The cursor is being used to modify the left-hand side of the 'stand-off', the area around the circle from which text is excluded. The right-hand side has already been done. Note the windowshade handle just underneath the text. The vertical dotted lines each side of the text are column guides.

PageMaker

Aldus PageMaker was the first DTP program to come on to the market, and is still one of the most popular if not the most popular. Uniquely, it is available in versions for the Mac and the PC, with its files being transferable between the two machines. It is column-based and page-oriented, although Aldus themselves say that it works just as well as a document processor.

To use PageMaker, you first set up column guides – dotted lines that run down the page to show where your columns are going to go. Then you 'place' text from your word processor into the first column by calling up the word processor file and then clicking in the top of the column. PageMaker will automatically create a text box within the confines of the column. Assuming there is too much text to go into a single column, you have a choice at this point. You can either use an 'autoflow' tool that will put all the text into successive columns for you, or you can do the job manually. This gives you greater freedom of choice over just where to place text.

Once the text is in place, it can be moved or reformatted with ease. At the top and bottom of each box is a device called a 'windowshade'. This allows you to 'roll up' the box, either simply to shorten it (to make space for an illustration, for example) or to move it elsewhere entirely. It is also possible to change the width of the box at any time.

Illustrations are treated in much the same way. Having selected the illustration you wish to import, simply click where you want its top left-hand corner to go, and the program will do the rest. Once it is in place, you can change its size or shape. Only very simple drawing tools are built into the program itself; just enough to draw a rule or create a tint panel.

The ethos of the program generally is that you create both text and graphics with other packages and then import them. It is possible to type text directly on to the page, but essential editing facilities such as 'find and replace' are missing, as is a spelling checker.

PageMaker has been steadily developed since it was first published. The current version offers such advanced features as automatic 'spot'-colour separation, which can save you both time and money when it comes to giving your manuscript to the printer. Even with only a monochrome screen, it is possible to specify the colour of either text or an object. You can use one of several systems including specifying degrees of either red, green and blue or cyan, magenta, yellow and black or Pantone colours (see page 181).

Another PageMaker feature worthy of note is 'wrap-around'. This effect allows text to come close to an illustration without going over it, although if the illustration is not rectangular, this requires quite a lot of fiddly editing. PageMaker also has built-in features for handling scanned-in photographs. It can crop, shrink or enlarge them as well as change the brightness and contrast.

All in all, PageMaker is a very sound and professionally-produced program which will serve you well if you decide to go the column-oriented route.

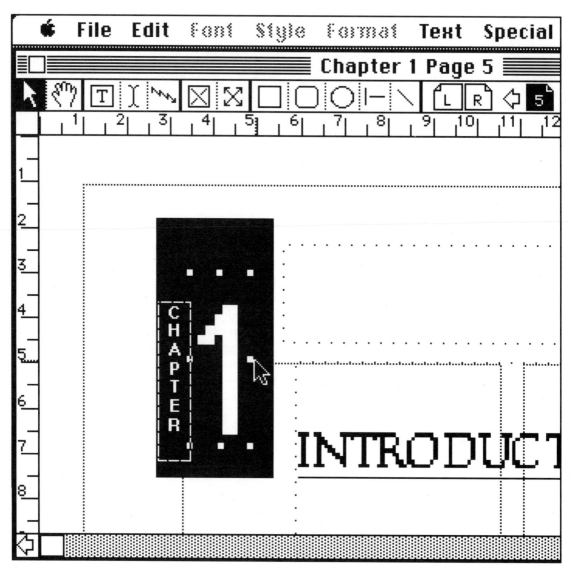

Screen dump from Ready,Set,Go! showing the headline of Chapter 1 of this book. The chapter logo is made up of three parts: a black tint panel; the word 'chapter' in a text box by itself and centred within the text box; the number '1' which is treated as a graphics object within the text in order to compress it. The fine dotted lines on screen are the grid, whilst the coarse dotted lines are the text boxes.

Ready,Set,Go!

RSG! is PageMaker's nearest competitor in the Macintosh market, and, whilst much less successful commercially, it is in many ways more powerful while costing about the same. It is a purely grid-based, page-oriented package, and its uniqueness lies in the fact that, while remaining possibly the easiest DTP package to use, it still has immense flexibility of layout.

Whereas, in PageMaker, text boxes are created automatically by importing text into the document, in RSG! you create them manually, and put the text in later - either by importing it or by typing it in direct.

Each new page you create can either copy the layout of the page before or have a totally new one. Creation of text boxes is speeded greatly by a powerful 'snap-to' function, whereby a text or graphic box will move out exactly to fill a box on the predefined grid. Snap-to is not unique to RSG!, but on other packages it only works within a certain distance of the column guides.

It is not only the layout method that makes RSG! different from PageMaker. RSG! also contains a full-feature word processor with all the find and replace, spelling check (American, unfortunately) and hyphenation features you might want. The only serious omission is a word counter.

The word processing feature makes it possible to use the program for such simple tasks as writing letters. While this may seem a little mundane for such a powerful program,
it is actually extremely useful. RSG!'s layout features can be used to create and print the letterheading at the same time as the rest of the letter, thus making it economic to create a new letterhead for each new project.

The program has obviously been created by and for graphic designers. As well as the grid-based approach, it has two main strengths. It has a major strength in typographical control. As well as the usual features of font, size, etc, it is possible to specify the space between individual words and letters to 1/1000 of a point, and to shift text up or down by 1/100 of a point. This makes very subtle layout changes possible, although actually making them look right can be very time consuming!

Like PageMaker, RSG! can produce colour output or separations in a variety of formats. It too has a wrap-around facility, in this case an automatic one capable of flowing text around any shape of outline without the need for manual adjustment.

The only real drawback to the program is that it has a history of technical problems. Particularly if you want to typeset from it, you need to find a typesetter who really knows the program and can get round glitches when they appear.

RSG! will suit you if you already think about your document in graphical terms. It is also your best choice if, like us, you prefer to type straight into your layout, rather than moving text around from program to program.

Quark XPress

XPress is *the* designers' or typographers' layout program. It represents the state of the art in page makeup, staying at least a year ahead of Ready,Set,Go! in terms of features. Like RSG!, it is a grid-based, page-oriented package. The difference is that it is more expensive, unbelievably feature-packed and much harder to learn. Perhaps as much because of this as because of its features, once learned it is also your passport into the exclusive professional DTP community.

Although grid-based, XPress does not seem quite as committed to the concept as RSG!. Its guidelines demark columns on the page without encouraging any particular vertical division. However, you can use these as guides to draw text boxes. The first surprise comes when you discover that you can create multiple columns within each box. Boxes may also contain subsidiary boxes of their own, so the whole thing becomes a sort of electronic Russian Doll.

It is once your text is in place, however, that the gasps of wonder are likely to come. The degree of control that you have over its final appearance is quite simply staggering. Not only can you control the space between lines, words and letters, but you can even control the width of the letters themselves. Not only can you choose whether or not to let the program hyphenate words for you, you can tell it exactly where, when and how to make the decision to hyphenate or not.

This level of control could obviously become very time-consuming to manage. XPress resolves this problem by using comprehensive style sheets. These allow you to set the font, weight, leading etc of a block of text, and define this as a style such as Main Heading. You can then apply all these parameters as a group to another block of text by simply calling up the style Main Heading.

Like all layout programs, XPress has limited graphics facilities built in. The difference is that Quark's idea of 'limited' is rather more ambitious than most people's. For example, it is possible to place a simple or complex frame round any text box, including sophisticated PostScript patterns. Other programs currently offer only either very simple frames or patterns that print out as coarse dot images.

One feature of the program that currently differentiates it from any other layout program is its colour handling. XPress can work in full colour, both on screen and in its output. Even colour photographs can be scanned in and electronically pasted into the text. XPress will then print out either 'spot' colour overlays or full, four-colour separations, including half-tones. This would otherwise be a very time-consuming process. The drawback, of course, is that to make use of these kinds of features you need a colour Macintosh, a colour scanner, a colour PostScript printer for proofing and a typesetting machine. We estimate that all this will cost you about £50,000 - perhaps a little too much for the parish magazine! Even using these facilities at a bureau is going to be very costly.

XPress is the most powerful, and the most expensive, layout package available, and it is likely to remain so. It really is a graphics professional's tool; unless you really need all these facilities, a simpler, cheaper package may suit you better.

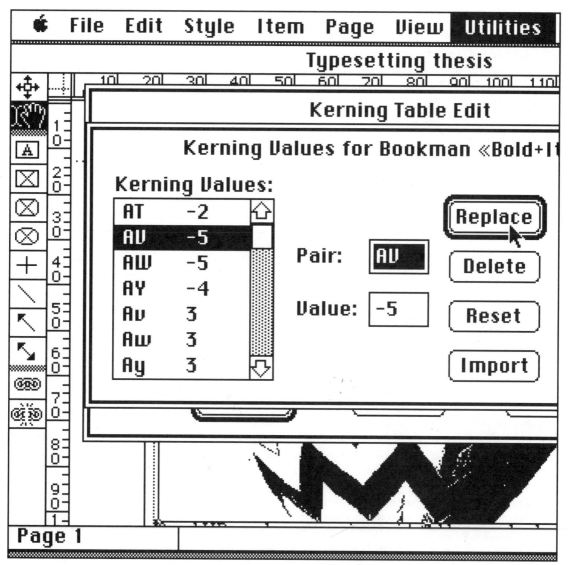

Screen dump from Quark XPress, showing a kerning table. Here we are changing the kerning values of a pair of letters; A and V will be moved together consistently throughout the document in places where the text is set in Bookman Bold Italic. The units are 1/200th of an em space (width of a letter 'm'), so in this case 'V' will be moved 5/200 of an em closer to 'A' than to other letters.

Ventura

Xerox Ventura Publisher is a pure document processor and is column-based. It was originally launched exclusively for the PC, but is now available for the Mac as well. It is designed specifically for the corporate market, to be a 'general purpose finishing tool across all applications'. In other words you are not expected to create your document in Ventura; rather Ventura concerns itself solely with taking your original work and improving its presentation.

Xerox's secret seems to be that, as a well-established multi-national corporation (one of the few to enter the DTP market from that position), they realise the need for a document processor that gives speed and efficiency while not demanding that you be a design artist or typesetter in order to use it. So this is a program for business people, not graphic designers. Since there are more business people than graphic designers in the world, it is not surprising that it is outselling all other PC DTP software.

The basic idea behind Ventura is that, rather than create a separate file for a document that has already been typed in, all one needs to do is add little packets of information about typestyle and layout (called tags) to the original word processor file. This file can then be printed out by a program that uses these tags to place text in the correct style in the correct layout.

This avoids the problem of cluttering the computer's hard disc with several files in different formats and at different stages in the editing process. It also avoids the problem of trying to edit text that is in a size or font that is hard to read on screen - in Ventura, you simply don't. To make major changes, you have to go back to the word processor to edit. Ventura does allow some editing from within the program, but it clearly doesn't like it.

To help interpret the tags, Ventura also creates a separate file called a style sheet. The style sheet contains two kinds of information. Firstly, it defines each tag, so 'bodytext' will be interpreted as 'Times Roman 12 point on 14 point with 7 point paragraph spacing, a 0.5 cm paragraph indent and tab stops set at 0.5 and 1.5 cm.' Secondly, it contains layout information, the position of text and graphic boxes and of rules or tint boxes.

One style sheet can affect several documents or chapters which make up a publication. Its users are likely to be creating long, multi-chapter publications, so Ventura allows you to create indexes and renumber pages across the entire set. This sort of power is not available on any of the other popular packages.

Xerox recently launched an add-on to the program called Professional Extension. This adds the ability to produce complex equations involving type of different sizes and fonts (including Greek), at different heights above and below the baseline. It also makes possible mail-merge type functions that can produce a number of similar documents each with different information. The ideal use for this would be a professional directory that uses a complex layout for repetitive information.

If you need pure document processing software that is compatible across the two major systems, then choose Ventura.

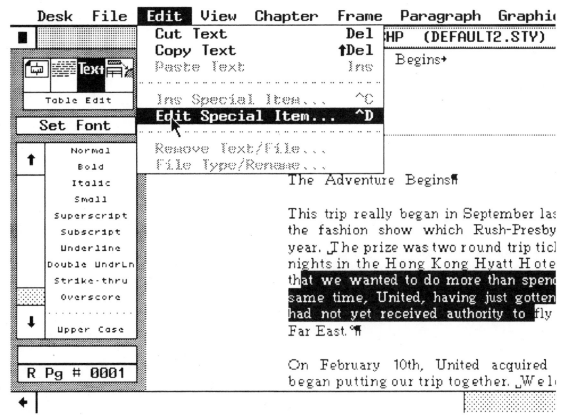

Screen dump from Ventura showing selected text. Ventura can be set so that menus stay open without you needing to hold down the mouse button. The table on the left-hand side of the screen changes according to the function you are using and is shown here allowing us to change the selected text (shown as white on black) to one of the styles on the list.

Calamus

Calamus is a grid-based, page-oriented package for the Atari ST. It is an example of the new wave of excellent, German-written Atari software that has recently started to come into this country. It will run on any ST with a megabyte or more of memory.

The program is the only page makeup package covered in this book that cannot produce PostScript output. However, as far as type is concerned, it makes up for this by having its own outline font system using fonts from the highly regarded Compugraphic Type Library. Better still, Calamus uses these outlines to create the fonts you see on screen. As a result, they are legible at any size. On Mac and PC packages, only fonts of certain pre-set sizes are really easy to read on screen. This is set to change on larger machines, either through the addition of their own screen-font scaling routines or through Display PostScript, an enhancement to ordinary PostScript that makes the screen look more like the final printed output.

Another valuable feature of the program's font handling is the way that letters fit together. As explained in Chapter 7, it is important to maintain an even space between one letter of a word and the next. This is especially problematic in larger sizes, where letters often need to nestle together or 'kern'. Rather than simply recording the overall width of a letter and then having to set up special 'kerning tables' as other programs do, Calamus inserts a notional border around each letter that follows its shape and automatically moves letters together so that the borders touch. This makes it especially versatile with non-Roman fonts such as

Gujarati, which require letters to touch or overlap. Our screen example shows several Asian fonts mixed together with Times Roman 'T', not a real-world situation but one that demonstrates the program's versatility.

In use, Calamus relies less on menus than on a bank of icons on the left-hand side of the screen. These are arranged hierarchically; clicking on one of the top icons will call up a different bank of them below. However, this approach eats into precious screen space.

A rather better thought-out feature is the text editor. In page makeup, text is frequently illegible on screen either because it has been scaled down so as to show the whole page or because a hard-to-read typeface is being used. One solution is to edit on a word processor and then import text back into the main document, but this is very slow. Calamus gets round this by having its own built-in non-WYSIWYG text editor. Click on the typewriter icon and the text in the current box will appear in a separate window in front of the main document. You can check and change the words before putting them back.

Text cannot wrap around graphic objects other than squares, but it can be rotated to any angle. Other text functions are hyphenation and indexing.

Finally, Calamus produces good output even on a 24-pin, dot-matrix printer, and excellent output from a laser. The only thing it can't do is print through a typesetting machine. Unlike the Macintosh offerings, it won't take you into the world of professional publishing, but if you are already an Atari owner, or if you are looking for a solid, little workhorse to run your low-budget magazine, this could well be the one for you.

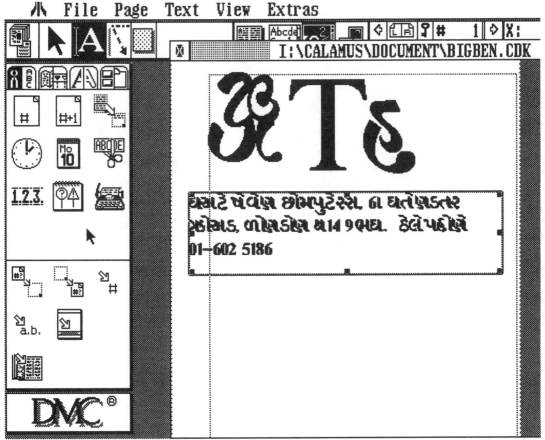

Screen dump from Calamus showing mixed fonts. Rather than using menus, in many situations Calamus uses an icon bar that sits on the left-hand side of the screen.

Magnified section of bit-map graphics showing limited resolution

Software - graphics packages

In Chapter 6, we outlined the uses for computer art. In this section we explore graphics packages, the programs that create this art. Graphics packages don't simply give us computer art. They also give us ways to design, create and manipulate anything that is not straight text - by creating diagrams and charts; by inserting boxes, rules and shading; by using a scanner to enter drawings or photographs; sometimes by allowing the setting up of colour separation.

Do you need such packages? It is possible to paste in all these elements on the page - and you may still choose to do so. The advantage of graphics packages is that, once you have your graphics in with your text, you can change them quite easily without having to re-paste. Reduction, enlargement, scaling and altering or shading are all possible on-screen and then all you need to do is to print it out.

There are two main kinds of graphics programs, bit-map and object-oriented. You may opt for both, or decide that one is more suitable for your needs.

Bit-map graphics

'Bit-map' graphics are made up of dots (also called bits or pixels). The computer stores the information about what's in the picture one dot at a time. Such software is often called 'paint' software.

There is a wide range of programs, with different resolutions available. What resolution you choose should depend on: your hardware - high resolution requires vast amounts of memory; your printer - a 72 dpi matrix printer will only print a 72 dpi image, regardless of the program; what you are planning to do - photographic preproduction requires super high-resolution programs, whereas low resolution is more than adequate for cheap and cheerful cartoons. You can improve quality even with a low-resolution program by creating graphics larger than you need, and reducing them on a photocopier.

Object-oriented graphics

Object-oriented programs treat each graphic as a whole rather than as bits. 'Objects' such as circles, squares, rectangles etc can be created on screen and subsequently manipulated.

The precision and control makes object-oriented programs excellent for technical drawings or anything that requires neatness. However, there is very little room for artistic expression in most such programs, because they deal solely with geometric shapes. Exceptions are programs that depend on PostScript; these offer very sophisticated drawing tools, but are more difficult to learn. Unlike bit-map graphics, the resolution depends entirely on the printer.

Many standard page layout programs include graphics capabilities, and we have mentioned these in the comments on pages 133-140. We now give four examples of graphic packages, two 'definitive' ones which gave birth to all other graphic packages and two 'state of the art' packages. All four run on the Mac, which dominates the field of printable (as opposed to animation or video) computer graphics. The one partial exception to this is Illustrator, which also runs in a cut-down version on the PC.

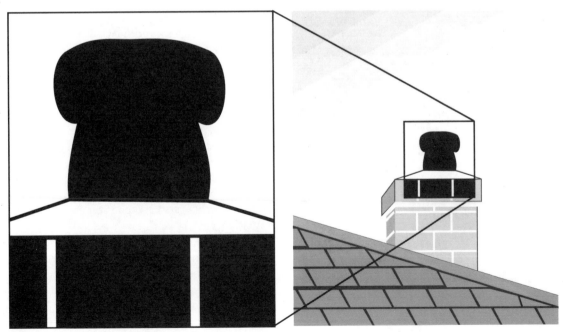

Magnified section of object graphics

MacPaint

In many ways MacPaint is thoroughly outmoded. We include it here because it is still the definitive paint program; virtually every make of computer now has several such programs, all of which use and attempt to improve on MacPaint's basic features.

The essential idea of the program is to provide the user with approximate, electronic equivalents of conventional painting and drawing tools. The artists' tools are shown on screen as a set of icons down the left-hand side. You click the mouse to select one and then use it. So, for example, the icon with a picture of a brush produces brush strokes just like real ones - except that you can change its size. While there is no colour option in MacPaint, it is possible to paint an area in any pattern (even tartan!), with simple brush

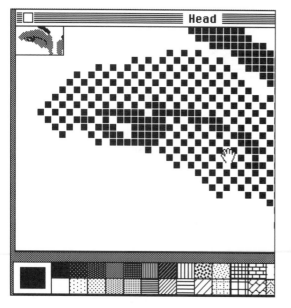

strokes. You can draw straight lines, rectangles, ellipses - and move any section of the picture to another location.

In the same way as an artist might use a magnifying glass to work in fine detail, MacPaint has a facility called 'fat bits', which allows you to change individual pixels within the picture. You can also retouch each little part without smearing! While it is very hard to hand-write with the mouse, it is possible to type - about the only time you use the keyboard with this program. Text, however, cannot be edited; once typed it is treated like any other pattern of dots.

As mentioned above, MacPaint is so successful that many of its features have become standard. So whichever graphics program you use, it is certain to have some of the elements outlined above.

MacDraw

MacDraw is MacPaint's object-oriented stablemate, and we include it here for the same reasons - it is a definitive program. It is a tool for a draughtsman rather than an artist, since it can produce neat, accurately defined drawings that can be edited element-by-element in the same way that text can be edited word-by-word using a word processor.

As in MacPaint, the mouse is used to draw with one of a selection of tools, but there the resemblance ends. Each object drawn is treated as a separate entity, which may at any time be moved, deleted, duplicated or changed. It is as if each part of a drawing were on a sheet of transparent plastic, and all the sheets were laid on top of one another to create the completed view. Drawings are built up from straight or curved lines, rectangles

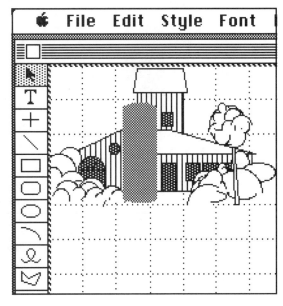

and ellipses. These can be drawn with any specified thickness of pen, and filled with any pattern from a selection of about 20 including black, white and transparent.

Once created, images acquire 'handles'. These little, black squares appear on a dotted rectangle surrounding the object. By clicking on one with the mouse, it can be 'grabbed' and moved, thus making the object smaller or larger. Similarly, you can change the outline pen or fill-pattern of an object at any time by first selecting it with the mouse. You can also move it in front of or behind other objects.

The influence of MacDraw has been considerable. Most layout programs now contain their own drawing facilities that mimic those of MacDraw. The way graphic and text boxes are manipulated also owes its derivation to this innovative program.

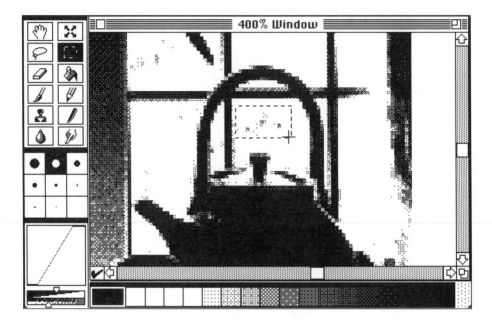

ImageStudio

ImageStudio is a bit-mapped package and hence a distant descendant of MacPaint. It uses the same principles to work at a much higher level of detail, for a very different purpose. ImageStudio's main function is to retouch scanned-in photographs.

To use ImageStudio you begin by scanning in the picture you want to work with. The program will accept an image with any level of resolution, even very high. And, although it cannot handle colour, it does recognise that photos contain different levels of grey, as well as pure black and white, and it accepts these as well.

You might then work on the whole image to make it lighter or darker, or to change the contrast. These conventional darkroom jobs are achieved almost instantly with a tool

called the Greymap Editor, which can also be used to create much more startling effects such as posterisation and solarisation (both normally difficult and time-consuming photographic effects).

Once you start working on specific areas of the picture, you can either 'airbrush' over things, or you can cut out areas of the image and paste them elsewhere - even on another photograph. It also allows you to create your own brushes, to create different effects.

All this power has its price. Although ImageStudio can run on a MacPlus, to fulfil its potential it needs the more powerful MacII, along with a high-resolution scanner and an imagesetter to print out on. Equipment on this scale costs tens of thousands of pounds, so most personal publishers are going to be using the program only at a bureau.

Illustrator

Illustrator is just what its name suggests, an illustration tool. It is an object-oriented drawing program, but one that is capable of results infinitely more sophisticated than MacDraw. This is made possible by PostScript (see page 152), which allows the program to 'describe' complex shapes to the laser printer.

Where previous drawing programs have been largely restricted to straight lines and simple curves, Illustrator uses Bézier curves. These smooth curves can form almost any shape, yet are simple to create and manipulate. The program puts 'anchor points' along the length of a Bézier curve. If you pick one of these up and move it, using the mouse, the line bends to accommodate the change. Each anchor point also sprouts a pair of 'direction lines' which can be moved to put a twist into the line. Shapes once created can be filled with simple tints, graduated tints or patterns that you construct.

You can either use the program to create artwork from scratch or you can scan in an image and trace over it with an 'auto-trace' function. This is particularly appealing where you want to create a poster-style illustration of an object; the photo supplies accuracy of proportion while you supply the style.

If the facilities are available it is possible to create 'spot'-colour separations and full-colour separations ready for printing, direct from the terminal. Using Illustrator, a good artist can create superb work in a fraction of the time that it would take using manual methods. Be warned, though, Illustrator *does* require skill.

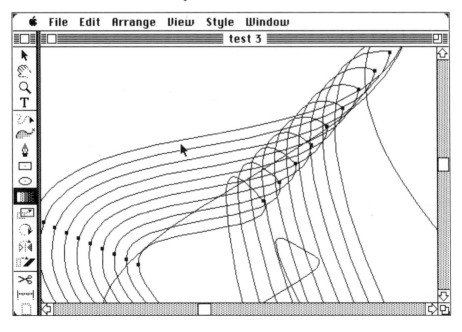

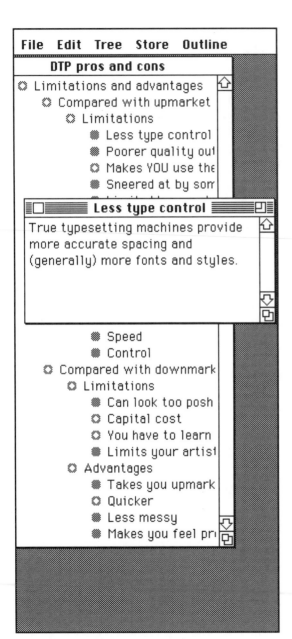

Outliners

As mentioned on page 46, outliners are primarily designed as thinking tools. They help you to organise large amounts of information into a hierarchical format, with headings, subheadings, sub-subheadings and so on. They also have a place as a presentation tool, especially for documents that have a complex, hierarchical, final form.

IdealLiner (for the Mac) is one of our all-time favourite programs, and was much used in the preparation of this book. If you open an existing IdealLiner, you are presented with a row of square or round buttons (little icons) down the left-hand side of the screen, with headings beside them. Click once on a square button, and its subheadings will be revealed. Double click on a round button and a window will appear, containing all the text connected to that heading. Unlike most Mac packages, IdealLiner does not offer a choice of fonts or styles of output. What it will do, however, is print out with or without numbered or unnumbered headers. It will also produce individual sections, or 'trees', to order and produce an index.

PC Outline runs on a PC without windows. Rather than having separate headings, it simply shows the beginning of each block of text until that particular block has been displayed. You have to be careful to start sentences relevantly - a good discipline in itself! On screen it is possible to open the entire outline to any given level with a single command, and also to cut and paste text to and from word processor documents. Printouts offer options such as different styles of paragraph numbering.

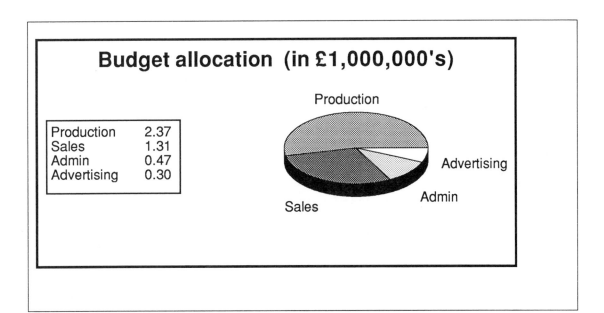

Spreadsheets

Spreadsheets are tables of figures; most businesses use them to calculate their finances. Spreadsheet programs recreate these tables on the computer. Once you have a computer, you are quite likely to use a spreadsheet program to automate your accounts. If you are running a publishing project, you may use one for financial forecasting and print scheduling.

It could also be that the document you want to publish involves numerical data of some sort, either as a table of figures or as some kind of graph. Few page makeup packages are very good at handling either of these (the one real exception is Ragtime on the Mac). One answer is to use printouts direct from the spreadsheet program, and several of them are now designed to encourage this.

The example we have chosen for the illustration is WingZ, currently the most presentation-oriented spreadsheet program. To create the pie chart, all we did was type in the figures; WingZ worked out the rest itself. The program makes it possible to present numbers in a variety of formats, graphs, charts, bar charts, all of which can add interest to a document. It may require a number of operations to transfer spreadsheet graphics to a page layout program, but it is worthwhile.

The program also has basic word processing and graphics abilities, so under certain circumstances you could produce your entire document entirely from the one program. The obvious use for this would be something like a weekly financial report that needs to look good, but must also be produced quickly, to a standard format.

DESIGNERS

CLARE STREET
Little Orchard,
11 Woodcut Road,
Wrecclesham, Farnham
Surrey GU10 4QF.
Tel: (0252) 733232
Jewellery (Precious). Hand engraving, specializing in seal engraving of heraldic and non-heraldic subjects and design for the latter.

EMMA J STRINGER
C H Goddards,
Aldworth Grove,
London SE13.
Tel: 690 6641
Jewellery (Fashion).

DEBORAH THOMASON DESIGNS
16-18 Railway Terrace,
Ballygowan,
Co Down BT23 5TL,
Northern Ireland.

KATHLEEN THOMSON
Studio 5, Lower City Mills,
Mill Street,
Perth, Perthshire,
Scotland PH1 5QP.
Tel: (0738) 38232
Jewellery (Precious).

GUN THOR DESIGNS
2 Boscastle Road,
London NW5 1EG.
Tel: 01-267 0842
Jewellery (Precious). Jewellery (Fashion).

ELIZABETH TURRELL
10 Buckingham Vale,
Clifton, Bristol BS8 2BU.
Tel: (0272) 72008
Jewellery (Precious). Jewellery (Fashion).
Silverware. Clocks and Watches. Porcelain Jewellery.

VIPA DESIGNS LTD
Chapel Lane, Somerby,
Melton Mowbray

JAMES BRENT WARD
16 Mid Shore,
Pittenweem,
Fife,
Scotland
KY10 2ND
Tel: (0333) 312015 & 01-407 2792
Jewellery (Precious). Jewellery (Fashion).
Silverware. Refractory Metals, titanium,
niobium, tantalum.

JEANNE WERGE-HARTLEY
5 Maisemore Gardens,
Emsworth,
Hampshire PO10 7JU.
Tel: (0243) 373586
Jewellery (Precious)

BRIDGET WHEATLEY
35 Stert Street,
Abingdon,
Oxon OX14 3JF.
Tel: (0235) 34283

Database publishing

Databases are used to store large amounts of repetitive information in such a way that it can be read, modified or added to easily and reliably. They are the electronic descendants of the card file that millions of businesses still use to record addresses or customer information.

It is often necessary to print a report containing all the information on the database, or at least a large chunk of it. The classic example is the phone book. The one that we have illustrated, however, comes from *The British Jeweller Yearbook*, a database listing that goes out to several thousand members. Obviously, the listing benefits from being properly laid out, a process that would be extraordinarily tedious if the publisher had

had to go through the entire document marking headers, paragraph breaks and so forth.

In fact, although it was not printed out direct from the database, production of the directory *was* automated. The publisher arranged for the database (in this case the very powerful Omnis) to produce a special text file containing 'tagged text'. These tags are very simple; for example, if 'Acme Gems Ltd' was destined to be printed as a heading, the tagged text file would contain '<head>Acme Gems Ltd'. The layout program (here PageMaker) is set up to read these tags and interpret them as style instructions rather than printing them out. In this way, only the final cleaning up of the report had to be done by hand.

Nicholas Saunders

With the increasing awareness of desktop publishing, walk-in DTP centres are now appearing in towns across Britain. One of the first such centres was the Neal's Yard DTP Studio in London's Covent Garden, which opened in 1988.

The centre was started by Nicholas Saunders, himself a highly successful self-publisher. 'When people read something, they don't just read the words; the way it's presented also makes a difference. DTP puts power into people's hands, rather than leaving it in the hands of only those who can afford expensive presentation technologies.'

The studio set up is functional and makes no concessions to convention. Sturdy work benches carry the nine MacSEs with their A3 screens. The central island reception desk also carries the laser printer, scanner and disc-conversion equipment. Studio users sit singly or in pairs at their machines using kneeling stools, an ergonomic improvement that encourages a head-up position - ideal for long sessions at the keyboard.

The studio has a varied clientèle, from advertising executives producing company reports to spiritual healers producing promotional leaflets. Jobs range from leaflets or CVs to 500 page books.

To cater for this variety, every machine has available all the most popular pieces of Mac software. Studio staff will sit with you supporting you to do your work, train you to do it yourself or simply point you to a machine and leave you to it. Unusually for a walk-in centre, they also offer a full disc translation service from the Amstrad PCW, thus allowing people at the bottom end of the budget scale to produce complete DTP work.

Many clients misunderstand what DTP can and cannot do. 'People imagine either that they will hand in a manuscript and get back a complete book, or, that if they do it themselves, it will take no skill. They take for granted many things, such as line spacing, that actually involve decision-making.'

As if on cue, to emphasise the point, an executive from a local company came in while we were conducting the interview. She wanted to re-publish a manual for which the original artwork had been lost. It took almost 15 minutes to explain to her that it would not be possible simply to scan in the old manuscript and print it out fresh and pristine from the laser printer. She clearly felt betrayed by this wondrous technology that seemed to promise so much, yet deliver so little.

Nicholas has used his own facilities to produce a pamphlet called *Publish*! (see Appendix) explaining just how to do what is possible, and avoid what is not. 'DTP is a tool, and like any tool has its limitations and must be used with skill.'

We would like to see many more such studios as Neal's Yard, most particularly because of the genuine commitment to open access that it represents.

PostScript

The whole reason that you, as a personal publisher, have a computer is to produce output on paper, so you are certainly going to need some sort of printer. We have already mentioned one kind, the laser printer, at the start of the chapter. In the following section we are going to list most of the other, available kinds. In order to understand what they can and can't do, however, you need to know about PostScript.

If you think back to when you learned to write, you will remember that you spent a great deal of time learning the shapes of the 80-odd characters (upper and lower case letters, numerals and punctuation marks) commonly used in written English. Similarly, a printer needs to remember the shapes of the letters it prints.

With the two exceptions of daisywheel printers and pen plotters, all computer printers work by building up the printed image from a series of dots. The most obvious way for a printer to store a character is to remember which dots should be printed and which not. This works well for straightforward printing of text; a simple dot matrix needs to remember a mere 45 dots per character while a laser printer copes with about 4500 - still quite an easy job. However, complex, DTP-style printing involves mixing different fonts, styles and sizes with graphics, all on the same page. The only way to cope with this is to tell the printer what the entire page looks like, all in one go.

Whilst still quite easy for a dot-matrix printer, for a laser printer this involves eight million dots per page. PostScript is a facility that was invented to get round the problem.

PostScript remembers characters the way you do - as outlines. These outlines can be scaled up or down, or distorted in various ways by a suitable program. Any other shape of any size can be added. In this way a DTP program can build up and print a very complex page.

There is still a catch; at some stage this outline-based description still has to be turned into the eight million black or white dots that make up a laser printed page, and this requires the printer to contain a computer of its own. This increases the cost of the printer, currently by about £1000, although, if the printer is to be shared between several computers, the cost stings a little less.

An alternative that has recently been developed uses the main computer both to create the file and to convert it into a dot (or bit-mapped) image, which is then sent to a non-PostScript printer. Systems that do this on the PC can take half an hour per page to print; the same idea is used on the Atari ST to print almost instantaneously.

PostScript output is only worth considering if you are printing at laser quality or better. If you are, then consider how much flexibility you need. On the Atari ST you don't need PostScript; on the Amstrad PCW you cannot have it. On the PC or Mac, a non-PostScript printer will limit you to a few fonts and very simple graphics, but these will print at just the same quality as PostScript. If you want the full versatility, or if you are producing laser proofs before going on to final typesetting, bite the bullet and pay out for the genuine article.

Hardware – printers

You will choose your printer either when you first buy your system or when you feel you want to 'upgrade' your facilities. These are some points to consider.

How to choose

- Do you need PostScript or not? The notes on page 152 will guide you.
- What kind of printer will be compatible with your other hardware and software?
- What page size do you need your printer to take? Most laser printers only take A4; dot matrix and daisywheels may take a variety of sizes.
- What kind of paper feed do you need your printer to have? This is only an issue for low- and middle-priced printers. They may take continuous-feed paper (which has rough edges) or single sheets. If the latter, your choice is to buy a cut-sheet feed (usually an extra) or feed sheets in one at a time by hand.
- What graphics do you need? Check the graphic capabilities of the printer you have in mind. How accurate is its reproduction of the wonderful graphics you have created? Any printer but a daisywheel can print graphics, but quality will vary.
- Do you need colour? Cheap colour printers can be fun, but will not do for professional work. Good colour printers cost tens of thousands of pounds and are generally used for proofing colour work in professional graphics companies.
- How much can you afford? Printer costs

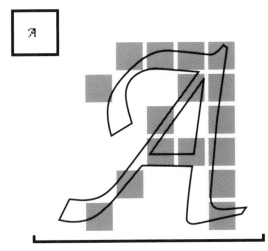

An upper-case letter shown both as a bit-map and as a PostScript representation. It is obvious how much clearer and more accurate the PostScript version is.

vary from 'free' (every Amstrad PCW 8256, for example, comes with its own dot- matrix printer) to tens of thousands of pounds for a laser colour printer. You may find it better to buy a cheaper printer for proofing and use out-of-house facilities for your final run.

What are the options?

Once you have identified your printing needs, consider the options. A 1989 survey in *PC World*, a personal computer magazine, listed over 225 brands of printer available today! So we are not attempting to list even a selection, but instead identify the generic types and what they do.

Laser printer

One of the elements that has created the publishing revolution is the laser printer, which prints copy with 'nearly' the same resolution as typeset text.

A laser printer works in much the same way as a photocopier, only, instead of focusing the image of the original through a lens, it uses a laser to 'draw' the image on to the page. The quality is excellent, although, if you want real versatility, you will need PostScript or one of its alternatives on your printer. If you don't have PostScript, you need to check what fonts you have on the printer you do buy, and what further fonts you can get, for what cost. The page size a laser printer takes will usually be A4.

Laser printers are very expensive, but their power and resolution usually make them worth it. Because of the cost, it is worth checking whether you can network your laser printer with more than one machine, thus saving money. You will, of course, already have checked that the laser printer you consider is compatible with your existing hardware and software.

There is a great deal publicised about speed of laser printers - how many pages it does per minute, for example. We reckon this is a red herring. Instead, find out how long it will take a printer to produce a sample sheet of graphics, and judge its power on that.

Daisywheel

These work like typewriters by pressing each individual character on to a ribbon. They are slow, noisy, won't do graphics and you can only get typewriter-style fonts. You can't change fonts without changing the wheel.

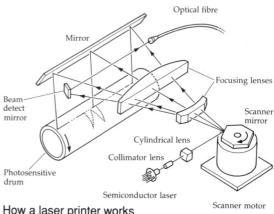

How a laser printer works

That said, the letter quality is the best, the standard all the other kinds of printer aim for.

Dot matrix

On dot-matrix printers, individual letters are put together by patterns of pins on a ribbon. Nine-pin dot matrix is not good quality, although some printers offer a near letter-quality (NLQ) function. Twenty-four pin machines are letter-quality (LQ), and will be fine for short-life publications or those that need a 'friendly' feel. You can get limited colour graphic options with colour ribbons, and some dot-matrix printers are cheap. However a dot-matrix printer can take an age to print, sounds like a cat sliding off a tin roof, and cannot handle PostScript.

Thermal transfer

This is a sophisticated version of dot matrix, using heat rather than pressure to transfer the ink to the paper. Another emergent technology to rival the laser printer, some now have both colour and PostScript. Also, they are silent.

word pro

scientific

Twenty-four-pin dot matrix printer

Ink jet printer

YES

The quick brown fox

Daisywheel printer

Nine-pin dot matrix printer

Please directly

First ideas are your document. success or failure.

Laser printer

On the top of Mount Moriah, got on well and worked hard to

Imagesetter

Different kinds of printer output

Ink jet

Ink jet printers (also called bubble jet by some companies) are developing rapidly and may soon offer higher resolution than laser printers.

Imagesetter

Another word for 'phototypesetter', this is out of range of all but the most well-funded personal publishing projects. It has super high resolution, but is troublesome to use, and is strictly for professionals. You can get access to one via a bureau.

Flat-bed scanner

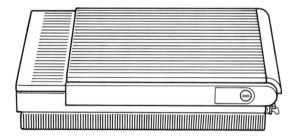

Hand-held scanner

Hardware - scanners

A scanner takes an image and converts it into information that your computer can understand and work with.

As such, it can be absolutely invaluable in allowing you to use photos, which would normally need special processing (see Chapters 9 and 10). With a scanner, you can convert these into ready-to-print graphics. Not only that, but, once converted, they can be fed into your existing page layout, positioned and trimmed to size. You can also alter the brightness of an image, delete sections of it, and electronically retouch it.

This all sounds wonderful, but has its drawbacks. Chiefly, the quality of scanned images is not all it should be. We have been known to abandon a scanned image in disgust and opt for a photocopy of the image. Scanning can take an long time, and retouching images to improve them takes even longer. Also, scanners are very expensive.

One key issue of quality is that of resolution, that is, how many dots per square inch (dpi) the scanner can record. The higher the resolution, the better the result. However, high resolution requires vast amounts of memory and disc space. Ideally, your scanner will offer variable resolution. To be more than a toy it must read images at least 300 dpi; more if you want to use it for enlargement.

The other key issue is how many 'grey scales' a machine has, that is how many shades of grey it can read. You don't need any grey scales at all for reproducing line work. For photographs, the ideal is 256 grey scales. However, you will need to use a top-of-the-range imagesetter to reproduce these. If your

The originals of these two illustrations are identical. The one on the left was scanned at 400 dpi and then printed on a laser printer. The illustration on the right was scanned at 200 dpi, printed on a laser printer and subsequently photo-enlarged to the same size. Note how the edge of the rectangle on the right hand picture is much more jagged.

final artwork is to be produced on a laser printer, 32 grey scales will be sufficient.

There are a number of scanner types available: the flat-bed, photocopier-like scanner, the sheet-fed, fax-like scanner, the hand-held scanner and the scanner based on a video camera. All have their advantages and disadvantages; hand-held scanners need a steady hand, flat bed are more expensive.

One thing to note is that anything you scan in will be stored by the computer as a bit-map (see pages 142-3). This means that you can't scan in a picture like a technical drawing and then manipulate it using an object-oriented program, or feed in text and then edit it.

The one exception is optical character recognition (OCR) programs that are meant to 'read' scanned text; up to now they have been inaccurate and unreliable, but we hear better reports of late. Certainly if you have large amounts of text to scan, it is worth testing out your nearest bureau OCR.

We would not recommend buying a scanner unless you have a large budget and use a lot of photos or tone work. Consider instead using a bureau facility. Many bureaux now have scanners, and charge per page. If you know one that is easily available and that is compatible with your system, it may be best to opt for this. Also, bureaux are more likely to have the newest model of scanner; with new technology moving quickly this can be crucial.

If you do decide to buy a scanner, check carefully its compatibility with your hardware and software.

Hardware – screens

You may be tempted to take your screen for granted; your system may come with its own monitor, the specification of the screen decided for you in advance, or the dealer may have a favourite and simply assume that you will be happy with it. However, as the means whereby you see what you are doing, a screen is vital and deserves careful consideration.

What choice do you have?

Any system that has a screen that is physically separate from the computer will offer you some choice. On large Mac or PC systems the choice is quite wide, encompassing a range of options of colour, size, shape, resolution and refresh rate.

What colour?

The first choice is full colour or monochrome (that is, one colour). Colour monitors are more expensive and in general undesirable for personal publishing; monochrome screens are sharper, and often easier on the eye. If you do choose colour, it will probably be because the system you choose for another reason has colour as part of the 'deal' or because you are going to be publishing in colour. Really good quality colour screens cost several thousand pounds, so get good advice before buying.

The choice in monochrome screens is between black-and-white, green or amber. This last is the most popular option. Some monochrome screens also offer several grey scales. If you are working with scanned in photographs a lot, this is virtually a necessity. If you only work with them occasionally, it is

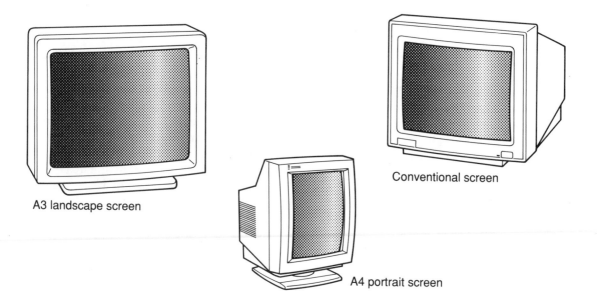

A3 landscape screen

A4 portrait screen

Conventional screen

Ordinary TV screen being used as a TV monitor; the poor quality can cause eyestrain.

a luxury, and for purely text and line work it is irrelevant.

Size and shape

Normal computer screens only let you see half of your page at any one time. Obviously, the bigger the screen, the easier and more effective your personal publishing will be. You can see all your page instead of a portion and you can make detailed decisions on layout without needing to carry in your mind's eye a picture of the whole spread.

The ideal for personal publishing is probably an A3 screen, which will let you see two pages at once (but can be somewhat overwhelming). The portrait format (that is, taller than it is wide) A4 screen will let you see a single page in one go, and is preferred by some people. Once you have established

compatibility, adding a larger screen to an existing system can be a straightforward way to increase enjoyment and productivity overnight. We would suggest that, if you are moving into serious, personal publishing, where you are spending a large proportion of each day in front of your screen, you consider prioritising a large screen over other hardware, such as a scanner, which you use less often than you do your monitor. Be prepared, though, to invest more than the original price of the computer.

Resolution

The resolution of the screen is the single, most important factor for publishing work, because you have to be able to see fine detail on screen. You will need a minimum 70 dots per square inch (dpi) resolution for layout work; anything less is very tiring to work at and may damage your eyesight. This resolution is standard on the Mac and on monochrome Atari screens. On the PC you need a 'VGA' standard screen, which also requires a special adaptor. Monochrome screens usually have better resolution than colour ones. However, it is your printer resolution that determines the final quality of your output.

Refresh rate

If you watch a TV out of the corner of your eye you will notice that it flickers. Good computer screens speed up the 'refresh rate', which creates this flicker, to above 70 Hz so that it is no longer perceptible. You should aim for no perceptible flicker at all when choosing a screen.

Emission

Screens do give off electromagnetic fields and small amounts of X-ray radiation. You may want to look at the possibility of a low-emission monitor for your system, especially if you are going to work close-up to the screen.

Which to choose?

The two keywords when choosing a screen are economics and ergonomics. Within your budget, get the screen at which you can work most comfortably for the longest time. If you can, when buying, spend some considerable time working with your chosen screen before deciding.

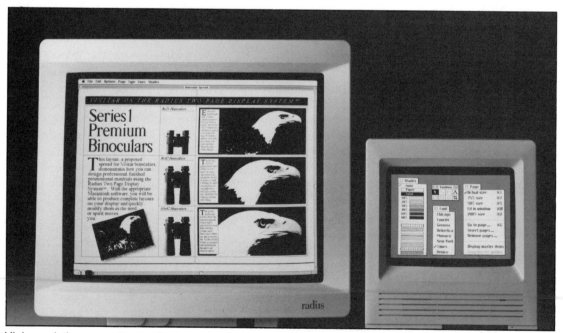

High resolution computer monitor; note the quality of the text being displayed.

Peripherals

Our illustrations on pages 102-3 show a 'complete' DTP setup. There are also a number of add-on devices, known as peripherals, that you may want to consider buying.

Tape streamers

All stored information is vulnerable to deliberate or accidental damage. The compactness of information stored by a computer, especially when stored on a hard disc, makes it more vulnerable than ever. A single instruction can wipe all your documents, company records, programs etc at a stroke - as can a fire, a mechanical failure or a burglar. This makes it essential to arrange some sort of protection. The most effective way of doing this is to make multiple copies of each file. You can do this using floppy discs, but because it is an inconvenient job most people get sloppy at one time or another. A tape streamer is a special tape recorder that can be set up to copy your data automatically on to special cassettes. The third option is a removable hard disc in which the data is stored on disc rather than on a tape.

Optical hard discs

Optical hard discs perform the same job as conventional magnetic ones, but they can hold far more data. They are based on the same principle as the compact discs used to record music, except that some kinds can record as well as play information. The discs themselves come in square, plastic cartridges; each one holds 600M of information. Their disadvantages are cost, though this will drop, and speed. Current models take three times as long to record your information as their magnetic equivalents. As the technology develops, they are likely to become the standard form of information storage.

Alternatives to mice

The mouse is just one kind of pointing device that can be used with a WIMP system. Others are joysticks, cursor keys on the keyboard, trackerballs, tablets and touch-screens. A trackerball is essentially an upside-down mouse; the ball is set into the top of a box that sits on your desk and you roll it around with your fingertips. They save space but can be hard to use. Tablets are plastic squares that represent the screen. You use a special pen to point at the area you want. Because they are very accurate, they are used a lot in computer-aided design. A touch screen does away with the need for a separate device altogether. Instead, the computer's screen itself is modified to sense your touch so all you have to do is tap it. They are great for young children or for public-access terminals such as the one described on page 205, but not accurate enough for DTP.

Modems

Modems connect your computer to an ordinary telephone line. This allows it to communicate with other, similarly equipped computers anywhere on the globe. Even the text of an entire book can be sent via a modem. Its advantage over fax is that, once some text has been received, it can be dropped straight into your document: you do not need to retype it. Its usefulness to you depends on whom you can usefully send text to, and from whom you can receive it.

The Independent

The Independent is one of the few national newspapers to be set up within the last two decades, and which has survived. One of the factors that has helped this newspaper to compete against its well-established rivals is its integrated, computer-based publishing system.

The new system, called Atex, has been designed to do for newspapers what DTP technology has done for personal publishing. Each journalist has his or her own PC which is used to develop, type and edit articles. Once prepared, these articles are sent to *The Independent*'s mainframe computer where they become accessible to the paper's editorial staff. They can then be edited and made up into pages - all on screen - before being typeset, also as complete pages. Very little paste-up is required; *The Independent* has only two paste-up artists compared with nearly 50 on one of its rivals' staff.

There is another aspect to the system that is of crucial importance. Because all the PCs are linked together via Atex, they can be used for internal messages. Editors can communicate with journalists and with each other about the size and nature of different articles, cutting down the time required for the enormously difficult task of marshalling the hundreds of different elements that go into a newspaper every day.

A particular source of pride is the integration of graphics into the paper. Serious newspapers are avid consumers of maps, charts and diagrams. At *The Independent*, these are designed directly on to MacIIs, which are also connected to Atex. The importance of this lies in the speed with which graphics can be produced. Graphic artist Ciárán Hughes explained that 'we can pull a map showing the location of a newsworthy event from an existing file, annotate it and drop it into the final page within minutes of the story coming in'. On other papers, if the map had come in just before a deadline, it would have had to wait until the next edition.

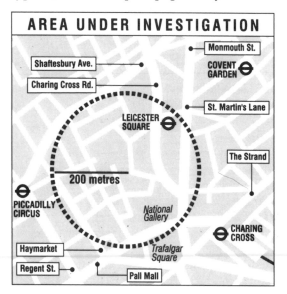

Getting the support

While writing this book, we talked to a number of people involved with the new technology of publishing. They all said the same thing, that your success or failure will not depend on your hardware, your software or your technological brain, but on the support you get while you are working.

Everyone takes time to get computer comfortable. Take this into account, and begin not by setting that vital job for the Sales Manager, but by doing a fun job that has no deadline and no penalty clauses.

Don't expect the problems - or the learning - to stop once you have mastered the machine. You will always hit bugs, and the best way to overcome them is to have a support system around you that will help.

- Unless recommended by a friend, don't rely on dealers or their courses to teach you how to publish.
- Some systems, such as the Macintosh, provide learning audio or video tapes. These are usually good and fun.
- Learn with someone you trust and who knows the system you want to learn. Get them to let you play and try things out.
- Take training courses to boost your skill only when you have built up your confidence. Courses vary from low-cost evening classes to exorbitant business seminars. Again, go on personal recommendation if possible, judging by whether the teacher's style suits and whether you can make useful contacts through the course.
- Books on computer publishing are often,

sad to say, out of date before they are even published, and magazines suffer only slightly less from the speeding market. But they provide background and support. (We hope that this book provides more support than most!)
- Radio and television often suffer the same problems, though magazine format programs can provide updates of the latest developments.
- Computer clubs and support groups, often nationwide links of people with the same hardware or areas of interest, can provide specialist support via meetings, magazines and bulletin boards (privately run dial-in information systems).
- Exhibitions are helpful to keep up to date on the state of the art.
- Network, network and network. Undoubtedly the best way to get support is to make friends with people who have the same system and interests as you, particularly if you hit a problem at midnight and want to talk it through with someone who will be equally fascinated!

For specific suggestions on all the above, see the Appendix.

9 BRINGING IT ALL TOGETHER

The text is edited, the illustrations are in. You will now need to bring the elements of your document together and prepare them for reproduction. These elements may be:

- Handwritten text.
- Typed or word processed text.
- Laser output text.
- Hand-drawn graphics.
- Computer graphics.
- Scanned-in graphics and/or half-tones.

If your complete, laid-out document exists in electronic form, you may only need to print out the number of copies required. This is a viable option only if you are producing very few copies.

If your master is to be photocopied, then all that remains is to number the pages on the back in blue pencil (which does not show when reproduced) to make sure they are collated in the correct order. If they are going to be printed, you may also be able to hand over numbered sheets to the printer.

But what if you need to combine elements – photographs with a page of text, an existing logo on a newly typeset letterhead? The image of new technology is of publishing pages complete, but in fact many documents still do contain separate elements, and these have to be brought together.

This chapter covers the elements of preparing work for reproduction, in particular the work of bringing elements together to form a complete page.

Who will do the work?

All the work described in this chapter can be done by your printer if you are using one. This ensures a professional finish, saves time and allows the printer to present the material to make the best use of his equipment. You could also get in expert help from a paste-up artist and someone who can screen continuous tone images to prepare them for printing (usually a graphics service). However, both these options are more expensive than going it alone.

Doing it all yourself can lead to more expense in the long run, if you misalign some text or misregister some colours. For simple jobs, however, it is perfectly possible to prepare work for the printer yourself. In addition, it is always a good idea to do a rough 'paste-up', using photocopies of all your elements, before the final one, to iron out any problems.

To the Head of English

■ Starting Points

A new way of approaching the challenge of GCSE - worksheet packs for GCSE foundation skills. Start students off with simple text and illustration, easing them into the skill and confidence level they need for GCSE. New bigger 40-sheet packs.

■ English Language   £14.95

Basic written and spoken skills. Topics include:
* work log guidance
* writing to instruct, describe, express, narrate
* why we read
* character and dialogue
* persuasive English
* oral practice
* surveys and opinion-giving
* projects and assignments

■ English Literature   £14.95

Basic literature appreciation. Topics include:
* why bother reading?
* constructing a plot
* understanding characters
* style, tone, figures of speech
* themes
* what are drama, poetry, prose?
* cross-media work
* course-work strategies

■ Core Skills Words

Now, more than ever, core skills are vital to the curriculum. But sometimes it's time for a lighter approach. **Core Skills** worksheets consolidate language core skills through the medium of puzzles and games. **Core Skills Number** are also available for when you need cross-curricula work. For middle school students. Topics include:
* spelling and punctuation
* reading practice
* writing skills
* handwriting
* speaking and listening

Out in September 1989   £12.95

This mailshot was put together using a number of elements. The basic text came in a single typeset sheet. Onto this was pasted a handwritten header, done with white chalk on black paper. The typeset pages were reduced and pasted in, overlapping each other, to form the artwork section. Finally a box rule was added by hand. The finished product was in black on white art paper, with red spot colour on the bullet points.

Preproduction work

Check you have all your elements ready. Text, whether handwritten, typed, word processed or lasered, should be properly presented. Your printer or graphics stationer can advise you about the best paper for your method of reproduction. If you have had your work typeset, it will be on bromide (photographic paper), which is expensive, but more forgiving than ordinary paper – there is no ink to smudge, for example. Check and proof your text well.

Illustrations will need to be checked too. It should also be presented on bromide or white paper. You may need to enlarge or reduce your illustration; further details on how to do this are on page 72.

Continuous tones, photographic or drawn, will need to be specially handled; they cannot be printed directly. They can be scanned in if you have a printer that will reproduce them successfully. We tend to think that the quality offered by most affordable laser printers won't do. If your local instant print shop has a scanner linked to an imagesetter, then take your work there. If you have no scanning facility, you will need to have continuous tones screened by a printer or graphics service. An alternative to investing in a scanner is to invest approximately £4000 in the necessary equipment to screen photographs in your own darkroom.

If you are using colour in your document, then your work will need particular preparation, often separating out the various elements that are going to be printed in various colours. Because of the accuracy needed, in general we advise that you get a professional paste-up artist or printer to do this work for you. However, given a simple job, where you are using 'spot' colour that doesn't overlap, you can indicate this yourself by drawing on an overlay (page 169). In addition, if you have the right software and some expertise in using it, the new technology can provide you with colour separations that are accurate enough to produce good results when printed. Some typical relevant software packages are listed in Chapter 8.

If you are preparing pages for binding, then your printer may need you to present them in a particular order, called an imposition. This varies according to the number of pages you have in your book, so check with your printer at the very start of your project. The picture on the left shows the order of an eight page imposition.

8	5
1	4

2	3
7	6

Avon Poetry News

Having moved from London to Bristol, poet Stephen Parr realised that there was no listing magazine to 'communicate what was going on in Avon in terms of poetry and performance'. Stephen, a professional graphic designer, joined forces with Sandra Stephens to found the *Avon Poetry News*.

They are now in their twelfth, monthly issue, with copy from 'writers, performers ... anyone who's involved'. 'With help,' Stephen types the copy into his Amstrad, keeping a consistent 36 character measure. This is printed out on his Amstrad printer and reduced at the local instant print shop.

Whenever possible, they get poets' own publicity shots or pictures from advertisements for poetry readings. These they have screened and reduced to fit, or sometimes photocopied. Occasionally, 'I do some line drawings myself'. Stephen adds Letraset headings to complement the Amstrad text, which of course is all one size.

It takes Stephen 'about three to four hours' to paste up the four page format for the newsletter. He does this two up ... so that the finished work can be printed A3 and folded. He likes to use a waxing machine 'because it's environmentally friendly'. The most important thing about paste-up, he says wryly, is 'getting it straight'. Text gets laid down in three columns, line and screened work is pasted straight down, and anything that needs reducing is given to the printer with instructions added to the paste-up to show where it is to go. The printer 'is very quick ... two days for a turn-round on a 2000 run'.

Although limited by manpower and the size of the print run, *Avon Poetry News* aims to reach a large proportion of the performance venues in the Bristol and Bath area, as well as bookshops, libraries and a small mailing list.

Funding comes from the Avon Poetry Festival and South West Arts, though at present it's not enough to guarantee the future. They're currently looking for sponsors and advertisers for the magazine, and are very hopeful: 'We're working on it!' says Stephen.

avon poetry news Free

Keith Jafrate "perpetually in pursuit of imaginative energy and the genuinely poetic" Roy Fisher

Keith Jafrate performs at the Arnolfini as part of the APF Summer Fling. (See listings July 30th)

Pasting up

- Equipment: a board for working on, preferably with T square or parallel motion; steel ruler; scalpel; light blue pencil which won't show up when the work is printed; fine-tipped, black pen; firm, unmarkable surface for cutting.
- Materials: masking tape; artboard or heavy paper, at least $1/2$ inch larger than the page size you are printing; if you are pasting up for an imposition, you will need room for more than one page. Adhesive can be wax, Cow gum or spray-on fixative. Wax needs a special machine but, unlike the others, does not damage your insides if used for too long. Test any adhesive; some react badly with laser toner, for example.
- Fix your artboard (called baseboard) to your working surface with masking tape. Square it to your parallel motion.
- Ink in marks indicating where you want the printer to trim and fold the paper, as shown in the illustrations below. These go just outside the print area so that they will be cut away after printing. It is essential that they are fine and accurate.
- If you are not pasting down a whole page of text as one, also blue-pencil in your original grid design, full size, to give you guidelines as to where illustrations and text should go. Often a printer can print up these grids for you at very little cost.
- Take each element you wish to paste and trim it using the scalpel and steel ruler. Leave perhaps 5 mm round the edge of each piece. Apply adhesive.

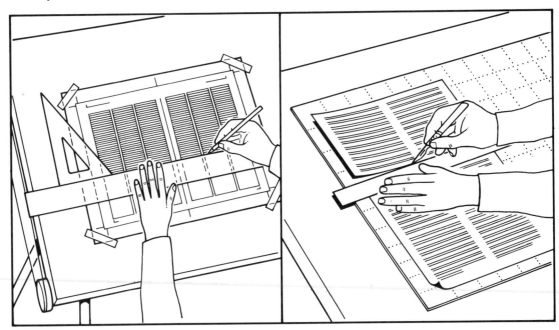

Pencilling in a grid design   Cutting text to fit

- Place the piece in position on the baseboard. For text, check the vertical and horizontal lines with your set square and parallel motion. For illustration, check if any lines within it need to be parallel to horizontal or vertical gridlines.
- If pieces need altering, manoeuvre with the scalpel. If they are misaligned, lift, clean them and the baseboard and redo.
- Once pieces are correctly placed, cover them with a piece of clean paper and rub down to make sure they remain fixed.
- If you are providing pages pasted up as they will go on the printer's machine (see page 166) mount them on board.
- Use lighter fluid to clean off adhesive from bromide. Laser printed pages smudge if you try to clean them, so you just have to be very careful pasting up!

Overlays

You may want to give special instructions on a piece of paste-up, to indicate 'spot' colour, cropping, placing or reduction, for example. Wait for the adhesive (and the toner if you are working with laser copies) to set, then attach a larger piece of tracing paper or acetate, folding the top edge over and fixing it with tape. Ink registration marks on the baseboard, then trace on to the overlay, so they align. Also ink in your instructions on the overlay, so the printer can see which piece of text you are referring to.

Overlays are also used for separations for the four-colour process. Creating them is a very specialised job and, unless you can produce them entirely from your software, should be left to your printer or paste-up artist.

Pasting down an illustration

Cleaning the work

Final preparation

If you are sending work to be printed, these further preparations need to be made. Protect your 'mechanical' (the technical term for work ready for the printer) by fixing tracing paper over it. Artwork or photos sent separately to be 'dropped in' by the printer need protection too, with stiff card at the back, and an overlay.

Marking up

Printer's instructions are written out on the baseboard or overlay, outside the print area.

- Number the pages in the order you want them to appear in the document. This usually goes on the baseboard and overlay, top right-hand corner.
- Illustrations not already pasted up should be marked with the page into which they are to be dropped. The page itself should show clearly on the overlay that 'Photograph A ... Drawing B goes here'.
- On each overlay, give clear instructions as discussed with your printer. For 'spot'-colour work, as described above, pencil in where each colour goes (for the four-colour process, we suggest you provide the original and instruct the printer). If any part of an illustration is to be cropped by the printer, show this by hatching it out and adding the words 'crop out'.
- Printer's instructions should also be included in a letter. Give: name of job; number of pages; size, weight, colour and type of paper for text and cover; ink colour to be used; any half-tones or colour separations; special effects; finishes; binding; length of print run; any drop-ins;

who to contact for queries. Many of these details will have been mentioned in your original briefing to the printer (page 191), but it does no harm to confirm them.

Sending off

Before sending work to the printers, tie up these loose ends. Do a final check on all your work. Does it make sense? Of course, if you spot any horrors at this stage, it may be too late. Then, check that the document is clean of pencil marks and glue. Take a photocopy of everything in case the printer has a query. Pack with care and many layers of stiff card, and send by registered delivery or deliver yourself.

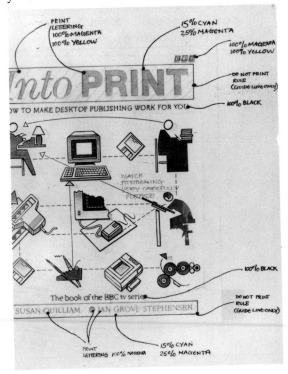

Curriculum vitae

When Geoffrey Quarry wanted to move on from his post as the manager of a small electrical shop in the Midlands, he needed a curriculum vitae to support his job applications.

Previously, he had typed up his curriculum vitae on a daisywheel machine and photocopied it for each new application. This time, he approached Roger, a friend who had an IBM PC, and 'leant on him heavily to give me something a bit more upmarket'.

The design the two came up with was essentially 'a normal list-like CV, but with added extras'. The added extras included the layout: a striking heading at the top of the first page with Geoffrey's name and address, and a box into which Geoffrey could drop a photograph of himself for each application. 'I think that was something a bit different – quite a few people commented on it when I went for interviews. It helped employers to get a picture of me before they met me.' The main text of the curriculum vitae was set in three columns, one for subject headings, the second for dates, the third for details.

Geoffrey chose Helvetica for the typesetting, using bold for the headings and to pull out the left-hand column. 'I knew that it was a standard face, nothing too fancy; but for business they want things to be standard.'

Helped by Roger, he typed in the text himself, and laid it out. 'I had quite a lot of trouble learning the commands, but Roger stood over me and told me what to do.' They used the thermal printer at Roger's office to print out rough copies until they had a design they were happy with, and then printed it off again using 100 gsm, white Conqueror laid.

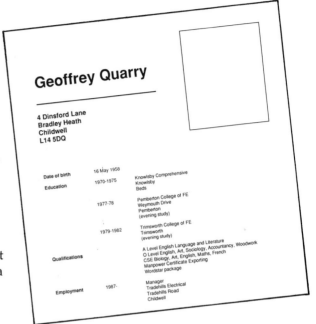

The difficult bit was the photo of Geoffrey. They tried to scan it in using the machine at the local instant print shop. 'But I wasn't convinced. The photo was very grainy and not at all clear. We spent ages "playing" with it, then dropped the idea.'

Instead, Geoffrey had a number of colour prints of himself done through his local photographers. 'I didn't use a station booth – they make you look as if you've just come out of the Scrubs. I had decent photos taken, then pasted them down myself on each copy as I used it; I tried doing a batch ahead of time, but then the photos got crushed.'

Geoffrey put his curriculum vitae in a plastic folder for presentation, backing it with stiff card when posting it. 'It must have worked; I got lots of interviews and ended up with the job I wanted!'

10

INTO PRINT

Reproducing your document is the final stage in production. The first decision you need to make is whether you will be doing it yourself.

For some documents, particularly those with a small, informal readership, it is often appropriate to do the whole thing in-house. A good photocopier, a set of slide binders, and you have a quick, cheap reproduction process. Alternatively, it may be vitally important that you have a four-colour run with stitched binding and embossing – but for this you need a commercial printer.

Deciding who will do the reproduction involves bearing in mind the cost, the skill and equipment involved, the energy and time needed, as well as your own preferences.

Which reproduction method?

There are many options available, and we list them over the next few pages. These are some issues to consider when choosing.

- Appeal: do readers prefer 'friendly', lower quality or 'credible', higher cost methods?
- Size of print run: traditional printing methods are cheaper for long print runs.
- Size of document: some printing methods do not easily print above A4.

- Turn-round time: traditional methods take longer, but may be less time-consuming for you.
- Quality: varies with different methods.
- Use of colour: unless you have access to an expensive colour printer or photocopier, this invariably needs traditional printing.
- Cost: in-house may not always be cheaper in the long run.
- Availability: what is accessible in your area?
- Special finishes: these can often only be done by a professional printer.
- Personal involvement: it may be important to do-it-yourself.
- Support: going to a professional may have spin offs in terms of the support you get.

Reproduction options
Do-it-yourself
Although the original idea of the new technology was that we could publish documents from start to finish, this in practice is less the case than was expected. There are still, however, many ways in which you can 'do-it-yourself', even down to the printing.

- Duplicators: if you have access to duplicating machines, writing or typing your copy on special paper or a stencil gives a cheap, quick method of reproduction. However, quality is low and document size is limited, usually to A4. An exception to this is the Risograph, a high-technology duplicator which gives good quality output but is not readily available.

- Photocopiers: an easily accessible self-publishing method, particularly if you have your own photocopier, a local instant print shop or a photocopier hiring service. The copier works by scanning the original, transferring the image to a drum and then using toner which puts the image on to paper. The method is particularly suitable for single sheet A4, though some copiers take A3 for folded work. It is also quick, and cheaper than printing for runs of up to 200. Its disadvantages are that resolution will be lost and colour work is difficult on all but very high-quality copiers. When photocopying pasted-up work, copy once, use whitener to blank out paste-up shadow lines, and photocopy from this 'cleaner' master.

These three illustrations show how printer quality is lost when you photocopy. Letters get lighter and thinner and eventually 'break up'.

Laser-printed original

Photocopy

Photocopy of photocopy

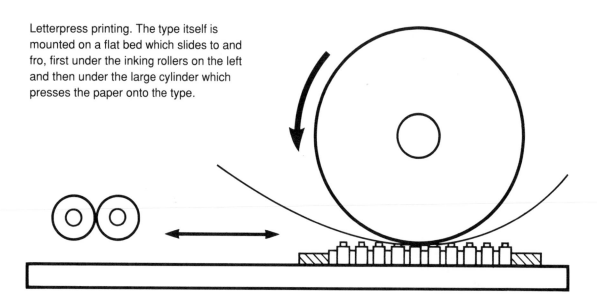

Letterpress printing. The type itself is mounted on a flat bed which slides to and fro, first under the inking rollers on the left and then under the large cylinder which presses the paper onto the type.

- Daisywheel, dot matrix, etc: these printers, as explained in Chapter 8, produce output of varying quality. It is usual to obtain your master copy from them and then photocopy, but it is also possible to use them for bulk reproduction. All the pros and cons outlined in Chapter 8 also apply to using these machines for reproduction.
- Bulk laser: equally, a laser printer can reproduce in bulk. It is expensive for longer print runs, and usually limited to A4 or smaller, and black-and-white work. Bulk laser printers are normally used for printing high-volume, personalised mail-outs. The main advantage of laser publishing has to be that you can customise your documents, producing them as and when you need, at the drop of

a hat, with specific changes for particular occasions.
- Any other ... lino cuts, rubber lettering, even potato stamps are all, to our mind, valid ways of getting into print!

Subcontract

The following methods are usually subcontracted. However, if you are prepared to input the training time, local community centres may have facilities that you can use.

- Letterpress: a relief printing method where movable type or a block in the shape of the image to be printed is inked and pressed to the paper. It creates high-resolution images and is particularly good for short runs, such as invitations, but is also costly and

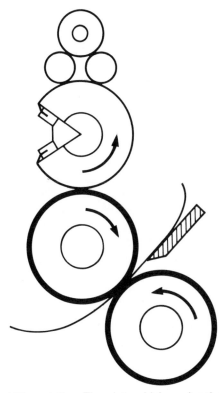

Offset litho printing. The plate which carries the image is fixed around the third cylinder up, and is inked from above. The second cylinder carries the rubber 'blanket' which transfers ink onto the paper while the bottom cylinder serves to press the paper onto the blanket.

not always available. Flexo printing is also a relief process, a variation on letterpress using nylon instead of metal, often used for small projects like logos, labels and bar codes.

- Offset litho: the current standard method of printing, where a flat plate is treated so that it has an image area that attracts ink. Offset litho is suitable for all kinds of colour work, and is ideal for quality printing of any page size. Unless you are using an instant print shop, it will need a medium turn-round time and, because of its cost, is more suitable for long runs.

- Screen printing: here, the illustration is transferred to a nylon screen to form a stencil through which ink is forced. You would use screen printing for any job where you need solid blocks of colour. It is particularly suitable for printing novelties such as T-shirts, posters, banners, badges, for printing light on to dark colours and for short print runs. If you are preparing work to be screen printed, make sure that the artwork doesn't include very fine lines, as they will not reproduce accurately.

When subcontracting, it's always helpful to check just which process your printer is using, so that you (and he) can plan accordingly. Some processes, for example, can take very fine detail, others can't.

Jonquil Publishing

(This profile is Susan's personal account of Jonquil, the publishing company that she founded with Phil Joester in 1983. Jonquil was, as far as we know, the first publishing company in Britain to move over entirely to DTP methods. It has given us a great deal of the experience and expertise on which this book is based.)

Jonquil is an educational publishing company that specialises in photocopiable worksheets. During our first lists, we worked 100-hour weeks and paid £250 per book for the typesetting. The second list was better, but we still paid £400 per book. Something had to change.

What changed was that we published a book on computers, and, as part of that, got sponsorship. We were given an Osborn – I suspect that, if that hadn't happened, we would still have been using traditional methods. At first, only Ian had any idea of what to do with the machine – the rest of us just gaped. It had a 5 inch screen, so we typed everything in to half measure just so we could see it!

We opted for a direct setting system that allowed us to set the text using simple codes. Soon, we were convinced enough that we moved on to an Apricot PC. Ian would cycle down to the setters and come back two hours later with something that actually looked like a book. It was a miracle. The typesetting bill fell to £80 a book, we cut the workload and the schedule by half, and we had so much more control.

The final transformation came with the change to WYSIWYG. The people responsible for this were our local Prontaprint, who had in-house Apple Macs for customer use. We started with a MacPlus, hard disc and dot-matrix printer, doing the setting through Prontaprint. We typed the text for each book into our template right from the start, editing to size as we went. We were totally hooked.

Another Mac followed shortly, although we held out for a year before buying a laser printer, because we could do that bit at Prontaprint. We experimented with scanning in artwork, but found in the end that, as we use line work, it's actually easier and less time-consuming to paste up.

The Macs had other spin offs too. The editorial accounts soon transferred to them, then the Sales Department got its own Mac, with a database program specially designed by Ian to handle the invoicing and track down bad payers, regular payers, and people who keep coming back for more. Of course, all the extraneous publishing, such as mailings, catalogues, order forms and royalty statements, is now done on computer too.

Our best move this year has been to get authors writing straight into the system. For two weeks, we gave Trevor, our health writer, free access to one of the machines, and he just came in with all his rough notes and typed his book straight into our page layout grids.

The overall cost of preparing a book for the printer has now, we reckon, been cut by 50 per cent though that doesn't include the capital cost of the machines. Our workload is easier and easier, even though the only subcontractor we deal with now is our printer. Most importantly of all, we experience less frustration – we know that, if it comes out right on the laser printer, it will come out right in the book!

KEEPING TABS

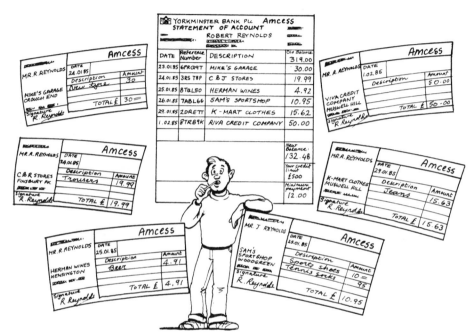

If you have a credit card you'll receive a regular statement showing how much you have spent using your credit card and how much money you have repaid. It's a good idea to check the statement against the sales voucher you have for each purchase.

1   This is your credit card statement. The credit company has made some mistakes in entering the information about what you've spent and paid. Redraw the statement with all the errors corrected.

Now write to the company pointing out the mistakes and asking them to change the statement and not charge you for their mistakes.

With your statement showing how much you owe the credit company, you'll get a payment slip. You should fill this in and send it with your cheque or postal order to the credit company. You can also pay at the bank, in which case you can use a cheque or pay by cash.

2   Draw a cheque and bank giro credit and fill them in for a sum of £49·50 which you owe Amcess. On the cheque after the word PAY you write AMCESS. Make sure all the other details you write on the cheque and giro credit are right.

Which paper?

The paper you use for your document will carry your message just as much as do your words and pictures. If you are keen to put over a no-nonsense, friendly approach, you will choose light, cheap paper. If you want to impress customers with your professional image, then a bond paper will be better.

When doing the reproduction yourself, go to a good graphics stationer and ask for support in choosing the right paper in the right quantities, to the right size. If you are subcontracting, your printer will both advise you on paper and buy it for you. You can look at, and often take away with you, sample books to help you judge which paper you need. Even more useful is to obtain sheets of papers and use them to do mock-ups of your document (see Chapter 4). When choosing paper, here are some things to consider.

Size

Choose the size of your document and the size of your paper in close parallel. The standard paper sizes are these: A1 594 x 841 mm (23.4 x 33.1 inches); A2 420 x 594 mm (16.5 x 23.4 inches); A3 297 x 420 mm (11.7 x 16.5 inches); A4 210 x 297 mm (8.3 x 11.7 inches); A5 148 x 210 mm (5.8 x 8.3 inches). Usual letterheading is A4, fliers are A5.

If you are using a photocopier or laser printer, make sure that the paper will go through your machine. If you are doing the printing yourself, ask your supplier for the SRA size, which gives you the normal size plus enough room for the printing machine to grip the paper firmly. Otherwise tell your printer how big you want the finished page size to be and he will do the rest.

Printers' paper samples

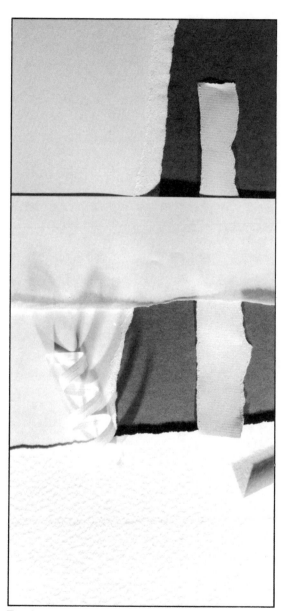

Tearing a piece of paper is a way to test its feel

Weight

Here again, ensure that the paper you choose fits your reproduction process. Paper weight is measured in grams per square metre (gsm) with a standard, stationery paper being 80-100 gsm and a brochure cover being 200-300 gsm. Heavier paper has a more credible, upmarket image. Lighter paper is cheaper – and also cheaper to post. For covers or business cards, board or a glossy 'art' paper will be more durable. Some 'finishes' that can be applied to papers after printing (see pages 182–4) will also add weight to them.

Feel

Remember when choosing paper that the way it feels creates just as much of an impression as the way it looks. If you can, get to handle a sample of the paper your document will be printed on. Identify whether smooth or rough, soft or hard, stiff or flexible is what you want.

Type of paper

Cartridge is the coarsest paper, generally used for envelopes. Wove paper is smoother, while 'laid' has a pattern laid into the paper by the wire screen used for papermaking. Laid is normally used for stationery. Bond is a heavier, rougher paper but very high-quality. For brochures or mailings, art paper is coated for a smooth finish. Cast-coated has a high gloss finish and is often used for covers. Some papers have a special finish to make them suitable for photocopying, laser reproduction or colour work. Recycled paper has a rough finish; printers may not like it because the dust it causes can damage presses. Take advice from the specialists, and get samples if you can.

Form

If you are using a printer with tractor feed for reproduction, or if you are producing stationery that will be used on a tractor feed, you need to order specially produced paper. The same is true if you are providing the camera-ready-copy for invoices that may come in two or more parts.

Translucency/opaqueness

You need to make sure that your paper is thick enough otherwise you will get what is known as 'showthrough', print on one side being visible on the other side.

Watermark

A visible watermark, while expensive, may also add to the credible effect of your paper.

Colour

Some paper colours, such as grey, have a professional image. Others, such as dayglo yellow, can be very effective for drawing attention to a flier. However, don't forget how many different kinds of white there are! Different documents for the same project can be pulled together by using the same coloured paper. Equally, if you are working with identical documents for different markets, using varying colours for each version is a cheap way of differentiating between them. Coloured papers are very effective for covers.

Accompanying stationery

Be sure to order any accompanying stationery such as envelopes. These can come in various sizes: A4 paper folds in three to fit in a DL envelope; unfolded uses a C4 envelope; A5 uses a C5 envelope.

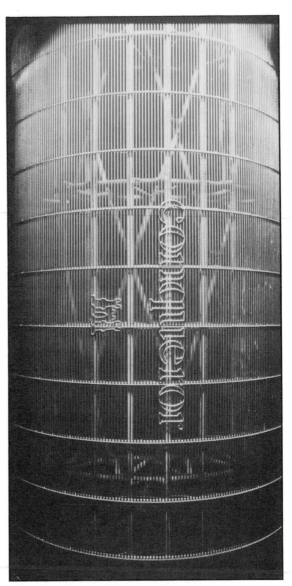

The texture and watermark of the paper are created by a dandy roll in the papermaking machine.

Adding colour

In this section we are covering a variety of media that can create images on paper. Remember that, in terms of reproduction, 'colour' includes black.

Ribbon

If you are using a typewriter or word processor printer to do your reproduction, then it will be the ribbon that creates the images on the paper.

Fabric ribbons contain ink which when struck by the hammers transfers to the paper. The ink can spread and smudge, giving a fuzzy outline. However fabric ribbons do last longer than carbon ribbons and are cheaper. Carbon ribbons work on the same principle as dry transfer lettering, so that the image transferred to the paper is sharp edged. This gives much better resolution, but costs. Make sure you replace fabric ribbons regularly or the image you get will become faded. Both kinds of ribbon come in a narrow range of colours, usually black, red, green and blue.

Toner

If you use a photocopier or laser printer for your reproduction, then the toner puts the image on the paper. Toner comes in cartridges and can be supplied in a variety of colours. While full-colour laser printers are out of most people's range, and therefore we are not covering them in detail, both these and colour photocopiers can sometimes be used at your local instant print shop. For both, be clear about the colours you want to use, but there will only be a small range available; consult the printer as to how to use them.

Thick printers' ink being spread onto the press.

Printers' ink

There are many different types of ink, but, unless you are running your own printing press, you will almost certainly not be making decisions about the type of ink you use for printing.

However, you will have choice about the colour. Pantone is the standard system and the 15 basic colours mix to make over 400 shades, so you have plenty of choice! Tell your printer in advance how many colours you will need in a print run (so he can choose the right machine), and, when sending him your work, indicate on an overlay (for 'spot' colour, page 169) which Pantone colours you need and where. The full-colour process uses just four standard inks to make up photographs or continuous tone drawings, so you do not need to brief your printer on this.

Finishes

Once your document is off the printing press, it can be treated before the pages are collated and folded. As with special effects, these can usually only be done by a printer – again ask for samples before you decide.

Machine varnish

The printed page is sealed under a clear coating of varnish. This gives a slightly shiny rather than a high-gloss finish, and helps to avoid fingerprinting. You might use it for the cover of a book, brochure, or any document that is likely to receive a great deal of handling.

Ultra-violet varnish

This is similar to machine varnish, but gives a high-gloss finish.

Lamination

The page is heat-sealed between thin sheets of glossy pvc. It also gives a protective finish, but is more durable, adds weight to the paper and is more expensive than varnish.

Encapsulation

The paper is sealed in an 'envelope' of plastic, which adds even more weight to paper and card. It is particularly suitable for restaurant menus, and we have used it for making promotional bookmarks which needed to be long-lasting and stiff.

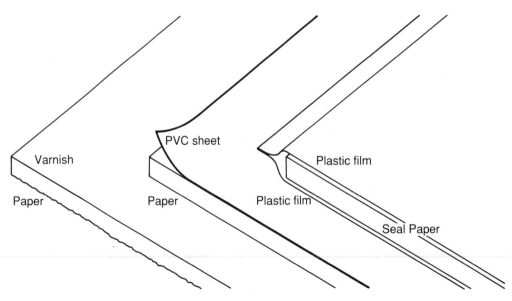

Finishes. From left to right, machine varnish, lamination and encapsulation

Special effects

As well as straightforward reproduction, printers can provide special effects that can add interest to your document.

Embossing

This involves creating a 3D image on paper by pressing it between two dies. If no ink is used in the image, it is called blind embossing, but beautiful effects can also be created by introducing colour in the indentation. Embossing 'invites' touching, and is particularly impressive when used for logos on business cards or letterheads. However, it needs a heavy paper to work properly, and is expensive.

Hot stamping

If you want to impress foil or metal on to the surface of paper, this is done by hot stamping. Like many of the other finishes we mention, it needs to be introduced sparingly, and it can create problems if used with certain tones. We would not suggest combining this with paper that will later be used for laser output.

Thermography

This process requires heat to produce a shiny, 3D effect on paper. It is again particularly effective for logos or any design where an extra highlight is needed, is permanent and lower in cost than embossing; it is often used on wedding invitations. However, it is not possible over a large area, you must choose your paper carefully, and it won't be suitable for paper that will later be lasered.

Production processes. From top to bottom, hot foil stamping, thermography, blind embosing.

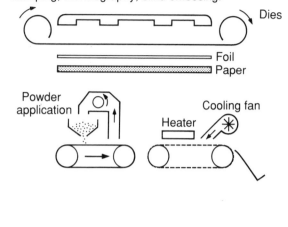

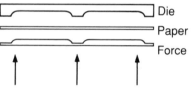

Die-cutting

A design is punched out of the paper in almost any shape. It can be used to create a 'window' on paper or a document cover, or to shape paper, perhaps by cutting out a nick or cutting off a corner. Make sure that the shape to be cut is not too delicate and that the paper you choose is heavy.

Engraving

You can have a specially made engraved plate for your logo or letterhead. It allows very fine lines to be reproduced, and generally adds a 'credible' feel to the image you present.

Shapes created by die-cutting, sometimes combined with folding and gluing to create 3-D objects. These examples are all standard catalogue items. Since the dies are aleady made up, they would be cheaper to use than your own design.

Folding and cutting. From left to right, folding against a straight edge, scoring with a blunt edge (here, the end of a fork), trimming against a steel rule.

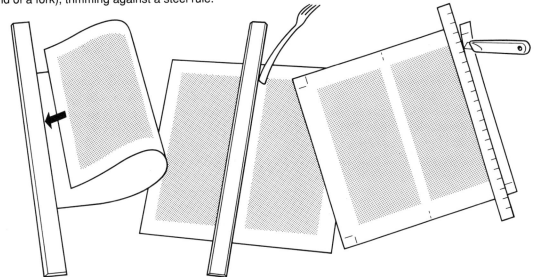

Folding

When paper is finally finished, the next stage is to fold it. This could be a simple fold, as with a wedding invitation, or a complex one involving 60 separate operations, as with a book. Professional printers use folding machines. If you choose to do the folding yourself, allow a great deal of time and patience, and always fold before you collate. For a single fold:

- Use a thick, straight edge.
- Push one side of the paper up against it, then fold and push the other side of the paper up against it too.
- Use a ruler to sharpen the crease.
- If working with heavier paper, score first along the outside of the fold with a blunt edge.

Cutting

Printers will use a guillotine to trim the excess paper away from each page, following your trim marks. Do the cutting yourself only if you have only small volumes of pages.

- If not already done, add trim marks to the size of page you want, using a light blue pencil so that any marks that are left on the page after cutting do not show.
- Choose a hard, flat surface and place a piece of stiff card on it to protect it.
- Use a steel ruler and sharp scalpel.
- Place the ruler over the printed area so that, if you slip, you slice into the margin rather than the text.
- If you are using a guillotine, cut a few pages at a time, and beware of the blade!

Collating

Printers will collate using a machine with a moving belt. High-quality photocopying machines, such as those you might find in an instant print shop, will also have their own collating system.

If you are collating pages yourself, the tried and tested 'round the table' method still works best. Place stacks of pages you need, in the order you need them, right way up and right way round, on a large table. Then walk around collecting and stack each complete document elsewhere ready to be bound.

You can have special collation marks printed on to each sheet when they are reproduced; these show you when sheets have been collated in the right order – and when they have not, and so need recollating.

Binding and presentation

Under this heading, we have included several methods of keeping your document together. When you choose which is the most relevant for you, think about the following factors.

- Size: how thick your document is and therefore how firm the binding needs to be.
- Cost: how much you wish to spend.
- Opening style: whether you wish to open the book flat.
- Durability: how long you expect the document to be in use, and how hard-wearing it needs to be.
- Document format: whether your format is unsuitable for certain types of binding.

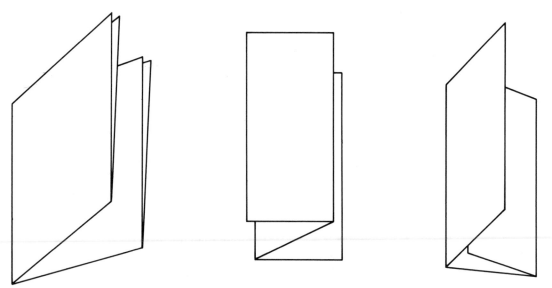

Typical paper folds. From left to right, cross-fold, zig-zag, roll fold.

Folding

A simple fold, for a leaflet or mailing, is often sufficient. Daily newspapers use this format and it is cheap and easy to do, but is only suitable for short-life documents.

Stapling (saddle stitching)

Folding your document and then stapling across the fold gives a similarly cheap and easy alternative, but one that lasts a great deal longer. You can do it yourself if the number of pages is low, and if you have a heavy duty stapler. This format is often adopted for newsletters, brochures or similar short-life publications.

Stitching

There are a number of different forms of stitching, usually done by a professional printer, and in general they are not as common as stapling for small, short-life documents. All the methods are moderately cheap and quite durable. Many stitching methods demand documents that come off the press in a large sheet to be folded and cut, so are inappropriate for single-sheet production. Side stitching binds single, loose pages at the margin, but in a way that does not allow the document easily to open flat.

Perfect binding

You will find this on most soft back books; it is usually done by a professional printer. The pages of the book are glued together before the cover is attached. Perfect binding is cheap for long runs and particularly suitable if you are publishing a book, or any document with a large number of pages. Documents bound this

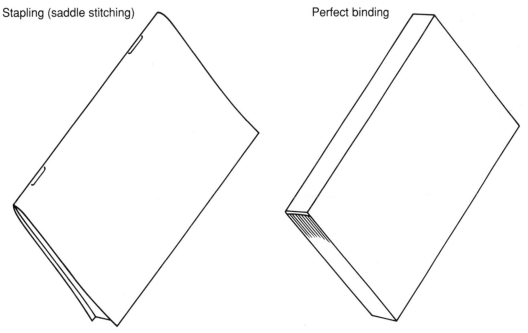

Stapling (saddle stitching)

Perfect binding

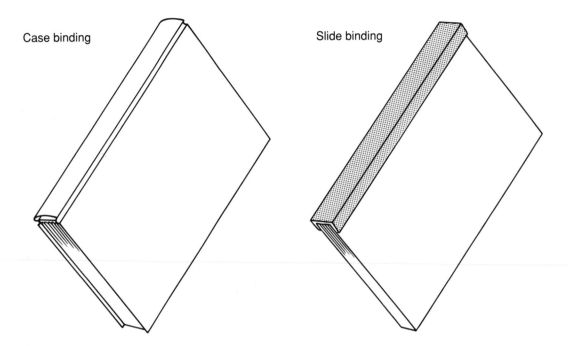

Case binding

Slide binding

way need to have their structure planned from the start so that the number of pages is suitable for the printing and binding layout.

Thermal binding
This is a do-it-yourself variation on perfect binding. Most stationery catalogues sell thermal binding machines and a range of covers that have on the spine a 'bead' of glue. Having heated the glue, the document pages are dropped in and adhere to the cover. The capital cost of this is high, but if you have daily use, as many offices do, it is a durable and easily accessible alternative.

Case binding
This, the most credible method of binding, and also the most expensive, is used for

hardback documents with a long shelf-life. Most printers will subcontract this job.

Slide binders
A plastic gripper slides down the outside of single pages to bind them. They, and accompanying covers, can be obtained in a variety of colours from any stationer or instant print shop. We often use them for presentation work, where certain sheets are standard, but others will be custom-made for a particular presentation.

You need to ensure that the left-hand margin of your pages is wider than normal. The slide binder option is quite expensive per unit but allows one-off documents to be bound easily and quickly. Make sure your cover and binder complements the paper and ink in your document.

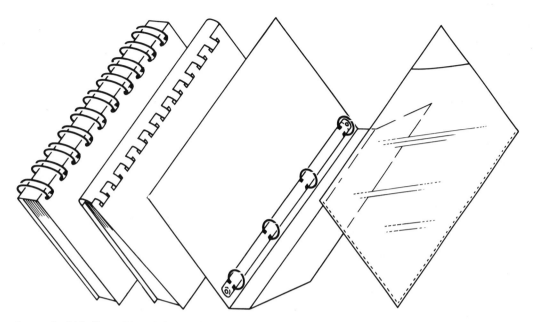

Loose leaf bindings. From left to right, wir-o, comb, ring, plastic wallet.

Comb, wir-o or spiral binding

These are varying forms of binding that involve punching holes in loose-leaf paper and then binding the sheets together with wire or plastic. They are particularly suitable for one-off projects that need durability, but also flexibility, such as training manuals, photocopied worksheet packs or presentation documents. Because they are ideal for single sheet binding, they are particularly suitable for DTP work.

All these forms of binding can be done by a traditional or instant printer, and it is also possible to buy your own machine. As with slide binders, remember to leave space for binding on the left-hand margin and to order covers and binders that complement the paper and ink used in the main body of the document.

Ring binders

For even more durable, single-sheet documents, ring binders are ideal as they allow the possibility of inserting and taking out sheets. They can be produced with your own logo on the cover and, though not cheap, are ideal for any documents that 'grow', such as those accompanying training courses. When designing your document, leave a 1.5 cm margin for holes to be punched and include the cost of punching in your budget.

Wallets or folders

Single sheets slipped into a plastic wallet or cardboard folder can provide a neat method of initial presentation for pages that will then be used separately. They are suitable for one-off publications such as conference packs.

Working with printers

There are four kinds of printer; large, commercial printers with many employees and machines that will do everything; smaller, commercial printers that subcontract work but have a more friendly feel; high-street, instant print shops with limited equipment and a short turn-round time; community printers that can be slower and less efficient but will probably take the time to be helpful.

Finding a printer

For all printers, word of mouth is always a good recommendation; ask your typesetter if you use one, or other personal publishers. The British Printing Industries Federation will be happy to recommend, although it is then up to you to check that the recommended printer meets your requirements.

For large, commercial printers, find examples of the best known, and write away for their brochures. You may well get a visit from a representative with whom you can discuss your job. For smaller printers, choose one in your area. We found our (excellent) printer by choosing six at random and ringing them with brief details of our job. We then went round to see the three most likely and, from that, chose the one who seemed to respond best to our needs.

Instant print shops have a reputation of having no time to consider 'serious' printing jobs. This is changing; if you have a large job, arranging to go in and discuss it in detail will often get you a good response. Community printers can usually be tracked down through local neighbourhood or resource centres, particularly those with an 'alternative' approach.

Choosing a printer

Remember these things when choosing.

- Price: a low-cost printer may not always be best, particularly if they are cutting their costs by giving you cheap paper. Instant print shops will invariably be more expensive, as you are paying for a quick turn-round time. Long runs of any document will be cheaper per copy than short runs, whoever your printer.
- Availability: printers have schedules, and you may have to wait for them to fit your job in. If time is of the essence, use an instant print shop.
- Reproduction quality: ask to see a printer's previous work to get an idea of standard. Once you have ordered, ask to see printers' proofs, a first sample of your job before they proceed to a full run.

- Special needs: all but large printers will subcontract jobs such as blind embossing and lamination – and charge a mark-up for them.
- Quantity: the longer your print run, the more reason to use a large printer whose large machines can accommodate your job at a lower rate.

Briefing a printer

A good printer is worth their weight in gold –
but they can't do everything for you. Don't
expect a printer to do the design, the writing
or the artwork.

Do check if they have facilities for
typesetting, reduction and enlargement and
paste-up, all of which may come in useful if
you are stuck, though they will cost. Our
printer, incidentally, has been known to ring
us because she spotted a literal on our copy,
and, after our shrieks of horror, to have the
line reset and dropped in – and still keep to
schedule.

Give the printer details of the following.
Normally this is done in writing, but if you
know the printer well, and have had
satisfactory jobs placed with them before, over
the phone will do.

- Basic format, what kind of document.
- Size of pages.
- Number of pages.
- Size of print run.
- Kind of paper – type, weight, colour, any
  special forms or watermarks.
- Any accompanying stationery.
- Number of ink colours to be used.
- Any use of artwork or photographs,
  particularly if they need screening.
- Any reductions or enlargements.
- Any special effects, such as blind
  embossing.
- Any finishes, such as lamination.
- Whether you want your work folded, cut,
  collated.
- Presentation form, including any special
  wallets or folders.
- How you will present your work; the

normal, ready to go version is called
'camera-ready-copy' or CRC.
- Deadline.

The printer will, having discussed your needs
with you, give you a quote (which should be
written) and a turn-round time. You may, as
we often do, want to get several quotes and
timings even if you have a favourite printer;
for some jobs, printers with special equipment
or expertise are cheaper or have a better
schedule.

Quality control

Printers will normally give you a written
quote and should not go above it.

Arrange a schedule with your printer. If it
is vital that they keep to this, put it in writing,
so you have a lever to use if they run over
time.

Arrange to see proofs of your work when
the machines are set up for printing and
before the complete run is done; a good
printer will make you sign a form saying you
have checked his work, in case there are any
problems. Some experts reckon that you
should try to be there at the print run, to see
the work as it comes off the machines – we
think this is probably overachieving!

The Modern Printers

The Modern Printers is a high-quality, general printing firm tucked away on an industrial estate in Edmonton. The firm was started by a husband-and-wife partnership, Colin and Frances Wilson, and is still run by them in the classic pattern of a successful family business.

About half of their work comes from other printers. A particular source is specialist, four-colour printers, who will often accept small jobs from their regular clients in order to build customer loyalty, but cannot do these jobs economically themselves on the big machines.

The other half of Modern Printers' work comes from local business and educational institutions. They have developed a particular specialisation in office stationery 'which,' Frances proudly boasts, 'we can print, perforate, number and even bar-code in one pass.' They can handle jobs from business cards (often still done on an ancient and beautiful letterpress machine, the most efficient way) to whole books, in black-on-white, 'spot' colour or full four-colour.

Although doing many of the same jobs as a high-street instant printer, the firm aims to provide both higher quality and lower cost. This is achieved by very tight scheduling of work. 'Setting up the machinery is what costs time and money,' explains Frances, 'so it is important to know exactly when you will be ready to send your work to a printer like us. We may have to charge you extra if you miss your scheduled day because of higher costs involved to keep to the delivery date required.' This is even more true of the more specialised colour work, where a group of jobs all requiring the same treatment will be sent through the presses together.

Although educating customers (and potential customers) is clearly something of a mission for Frances, she also enjoys the exclusivity of 'The Print'. She explains that 'the camaraderie between printers is intense – even when there is fierce competition between us'. And having seen the passion that these people have for what they do, we have to agree with her words that 'it is an incredibly interesting, enthralling trade'.

Modern Printers showed us a variety of samples of their work. One letterhead and business card set seemed to us to be an excellent example of personal publishing and professional expertise cooperating well.

Ian Rennie, a chartered surveyor in North London, got the idea for the letterhead and business card himself. 'Something in Tottenham Court Road caught my eye ... they were using a yellow triangle at the bottom of a page'. Along with his assistant, Ian developed the concept of the black triangle from this first inspiration. 'Adapting ideas from sources is what it's all about – as my lecturer at college used to say, "It's not borrowing ... it's pollinating!"'

The triangle concept got 'somewhat stuck', so Ian called in a graphic designer,

Mauritio Miquel, who took the whole idea a stage further, adding the reversed-out detail. He chose Univers 49 for the typeface on both letterheading and business card, using dry transfer lettering rather than typesetting. Mauritio also briefed the printers, which, as Ian points out, 'is often the hardest job'.

Modern Printers took over from this point, doing some 'general tidying up'. They printed the letterhead on Conqueror Wove 100 gsm and the card on 290 Ivorex. The result, still being used by Ian Rennie today, is the stationery shown below.

We like the simple but clear image which uses the sans serif condensed face for both the headline and the details. This is reversed out where it meets the black triangle and is emphasised by a thick, black rule under the address. Notice how on the business card this rule bleeds off, whereas, on the letterhead, it remains on the page, so that when the letter itself is added, all a reader's attention is kept on the page.

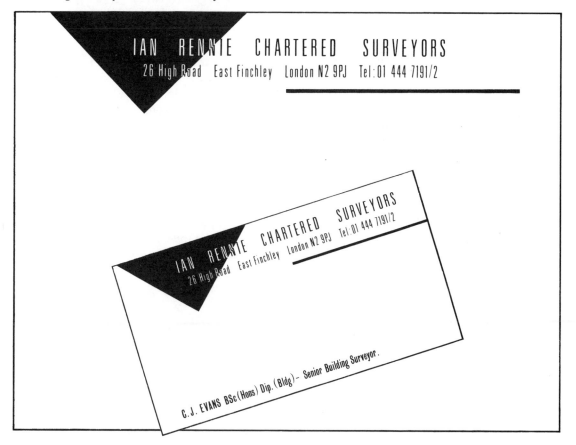

CHECKING YOUR PRODUCT

First reactions

Your first response to your very own personally published document will be a justifiable sense of achievement.

Your second response may not be quite so positive. The reality may not match the dream. The print quality may not be as clear as you hoped. For us, the ultimate horror was discovering, on flicking through our first personally published book, a 36 point header that read ACCCOMMODATION (three Cs)! Two editors, a typesetter, a layout artist and a printer had all seen it – and missed it.

Checking

Sit down in a quiet place and look through your document as if you have never seen it before. Do spot checks from the start, middle and end of the print run. If you used a subcontractor, check each one of your delivery boxes. Check against the roughs you have already approved. Look initially at obvious things, such as the wrong paper, fuzzy print, smeared ink. Detailed checking comes later.

Instant fixes

If the mistake is remediable in-house (you've photocopied on to the wrong sort of paper, for example), look at just how much money, time and energy you will use by redoing the job, and decide if it is worth it.

If the mistake is with subcontractors (at this stage, usually printers), then you can:

- Ask for a rerun: a good solution if there is one specific problem. If the whole job is badly done, redoing it will only result in a rerun of the problem.
- Ask for a reduction in price: most subcontractors will be open to this if you ask immediately the job is received, and before you have paid.
- Legal action: you need clear confirmation, in writing if possible, of what has been agreed at each stage. Seek legal advice but be prepared to be told that the cost of proceeding will vastly outweigh the cost of writing off the job.

Long-term quality control

Once you have sorted out the short-term problems, you will want to ensure long-term success by making sure your product is the best you can achieve. The most effective way of getting this sort of quality control is to get feedback on your product.

- Take-up rate: whether this be sales of your book or the number of people who pick up your leaflet, the take-up rate will show you whether your product is working.
- User feedback: ask the people who use your product what they like – and don't like – about it. Do this informally, or organise a questionnaire. Don't take everything to heart, but act on any consistent criticism. Professional market research is worthwhile, but expensive.
- Team feedback: you may well organise a meeting of those who have worked on the project with you, to discuss what could be better done next time. The feedback you get may well be about the product – but also about staff pay, deadlines, organisation, teamwork and the technology. If you want the best product, you'll have to address these issues too.
- Competitor feedback: if your competitor starts copying your style, this means that what you are doing is working – and also that you have to keep one step ahead!

Using feedback

When you have obtained your feedback, how can you utilise it? On the following two pages, there is a Quality Control Checklist to help you. When you have filled in the feedback you have received about each aspect of your

work – compliments as well as criticism – ask which areas of your project can actually be changed. There will always be some aspects that you are locked into. If you are producing a community newsletter, for example, changing it to a jazz review will not be an option for you. Mark on the checklist the areas that you know you just cannot alter.

Then, think about the action you can take. List any ideas that come to you. Could you, for example:

- Add more money: grants, sponsorship, venture capital, bank loan, fund-raising?
- Add more time: hire more people, extend deadlines?
- Add more resources: hire in expertise, borrow equipment, get more space, go on a course?
- Cut costs: reduce size, use cheaper materials, do longer runs?
- Produce it more quickly: cut down the size, shorten the deadlines, produce fewer issues per year?
- Rethink your production process: add or subtract stages, checks, new technology?
- Do something really original that we haven't even thought of?

	Quality control checklist
Product idea Was it appropriate for the market; was it appropriate for you?	feedback: action:
Words Were the style and the order of text effective for the market?	feedback: action:
Illustrations Were the style and the execution of illustrations satisfactory?	feedback: action:
Format Was the format appropriate for the use of the product?	feedback: action:
Document design Did the design work to create an impression and affect the market; was the typespec chosen effective; did it blend with the illustrations?	feedback: action:
Editing Was editorial organisation, copy editing and proofing effective?	feedback: action:
Typesetting Was typesetting accurate in terms of literals, placing, typespec?	feedback: action:
DTP technology Was the technology, hardware and software, easy and effective to use?	feedback: action:
Other equipment Was the other equipment easy and effective to use?	feedback: action:

Paste-up Was the paste-up accurate and stylistically effective?	**feedback:** **action:**
Production spec Were the following suitable: paper, ink, cover material, special effects, binding?	**feedback:** **action:**
Production Were the following produced as requested: paper, ink, cover material, special effects, print quality, collation, folding, binding?	**feedback:** **action:**
Packing and delivery Were the goods packed effectively; were they delivered to the correct address?	**feedback:** **action:**
Accommodation Was the accommodation suitable for what was wanted?	**feedback:** **action**
Staffing Was the number and quality of the staff (or team) appropriate and did they all work well together?	**feedback:** **action:**
Scheduling Was there enough time to do the work; was the timing of the product right; were deadlines met?	**feedback:** **action:**
Budget Was anything over-budgeted, was there enough money available; was the product priced too high?	**feedback:** **action:**

12

AND AFTERWARDS

What now? You have your document and your production work is, for the moment, over. Your publishing work, however, may not be. For publishing is about getting your product to other people, not just producing it in the first place. Depending on your product, this may involve several stages.

- Perhaps you have produced a document that you don't need to sell, such as a business card or letterhead. Store it carefully, and, if your master for reproduction is not with a printer, guard that with your life!
- Perhaps you have produced a document with a small, convinced market that is known to you, such as a wedding invitation or a subscribed leaflet for your special interest group. If so, then all that remains is to post the document. If you are dealing with large quantities, you may want to arrange an 'envelope stuffing' session.
- Perhaps your document has been commissioned, either because you are a professional desktop publisher or because you are publishing within a corporate or existing market. If so, the document will have been approved before printing, and all you have to do is deliver it. We usually arrange for the printer to do this, sending us a dozen or so copies for our files. Once we know delivery has been made, we ring the 'client' to check everything is satisfactory, and then follow up a month or so later to get feedback on whether what we have done has worked.
- Perhaps you have no need to sell your product – as with a free leaflet or house-to-house mailing – but you do need to distribute it. We give helpful hints for this on page 201.
- Perhaps you do need to sell your product – a magazine, a book, a leaflet. Because you are aiming to sell your product rather than simply distribute it, we hope you will have put time and energy into identifying your market and profiling them according to age, gender, what their interests are, how you could appeal to them. Having already used this knowledge to inform the making of your document, you will now need it to inform your selling. We look at the issues of marketing on page 200.

Joseph O'Connor

When Joseph, a guitar teacher from South London, developed an idea for a book about teaching music, he contacted several publishers. 'They liked the idea, but couldn't find a niche for the book'. However, Joseph 's project, *Not Pulling Strings*, received sufficient encouragement for him to take the idea further. He went back to one publisher, and got agreement to distribute the book 'if I took the risks'. Why was Joseph prepared to 'take the risks'? Part of it was that he had a project he believed in, but he also wanted to control the process, to produce a book himself.

One of the most impressive things about the way Joseph went about it was the rigorous editing process he subjected himself to. He contacted a whole range of people 'whose opinions I respected', including some university lecturers and experts in the field, and asked for their help in reading and commenting on the book. He got at least two people to proof-read every single chapter, and of course went through the typical author's panics of thinking 'it's wonderful ... it's rubbish'. In the end, however, he had a sound product, which everyone was pleased with.

Up to this point, he had been keying his text into a BBC Micro. For the layout, he transferred the text 'with a great deal of hassle' to a Mac SE. With the help of a designer friend, he laid the book out, page by page, on the Ready,Set,Go! layout package. He took his time – 'I didn't actually have a deadline in mind', though when preparing the work for press, he did only one rough proof and then a final laser printout.

When it came to reproduction, Joseph spoke to a number of printers and eventually settled for the one with 'the most helpful rep... mine was a very small book, but he made me feel that it was just as important as a huge job'. He had a print run of 2000, and priced the book at £5.95. 'I spent £500 on my headed stationery and office equipment, and £2500 in total on the book. This was £400 on the cover work, and £1900 on the printing – it should have been less, but I made a mistake and a whole section had to be reprinted.'

The selling of the book is largely dependent on Joseph's own efforts. He continues to call on his network of experts, this time to allow him to give publicity lectures about the book. He also goes to conferences to publicise it, gets reviews in specialist publications, sells it constantly.

At time of going to press, Joseph has sold 700 copies of *Not Pulling Strings*, and has just negotiated the American rights. In the market he is addressing, this is a remarkable achievement.

He is now working on a further book, this time commissioned by a large publishing house. 'I'm really glad I had the experience, but I don't necessarily want to do it again.'

Marketing

There are a number of ways in which you can publicise your document.

The first is word of mouth. Mention it to anyone who may be interested, in particular to anyone who will benefit by publicising it, for example the secretary of a special interest society. Find out where your market meets (convention, Chamber of Commerce meeting, parent/teacher gathering) and offer to speak about your document. Make the speech lively and low-key, but afterwards have copies of the document ready to sell and publicity material ready to distribute.

Whether it is your church fête or a conference at the National Exhibition Centre, find out where your market gathers and go there. Along with the document and publicity material mentioned, take posters. If you can, hold a demonstration to pull the crowd in.

If you have a document sufficiently media-worthy to launch, enrol Press help. Send a copy of the document to the relevant editor or programme director at your local newspaper and radio station, with a brief press release. Remember that the Press will need an 'angle' in order to bother covering your document. Also be realistic; national Press will almost certainly not have the space to cover what you are doing unless it is incredibly new or publicity worthy. If you are both author and publisher of a document, don't mention this if you are sending review copies – somehow, it still isn't credible!

If you are selling your document commercially, you have a number of options open. Mailings work when the mailing list is good, when people on it have already shown an interest in your area of expertise. Buying in mailings from professionals will cost the earth; slipping a leaflet in your local community paper won't. Advertise only where you know you have a good market, and haggle for discounts on adverts. Specialist publications are a good bet, but the cost can still be prohibitive – a mention in the editorial section will still get you a thousand times more interest.

If your project is suitable for bookshops, you will need to reach them. Go yourself, taking copies of your book, order forms and a great deal of goodwill, or obtain (at a price) sales or repping services, making sure that the people they reach are the people you want to reach.

Monitor all the above methods of marketing carefully, and ruthlessly abandon any that don't work.

REID ADAM COMMUNICATIONS
TARGETED PUBLIC RELATIONS

Tel: 01-480 5693 Telex: 885130

INVOICE NO.

Date

Client

Sales and distribution

Once you have orders, your workload will change – though you must keep the marketing going too.

Setting a price

Setting a price for your document can be tricky. Take into account the amount you can ask in the current market (look at other similar documents) as well as what you need to charge to make an overall profit. Remember that a retailer will want at least a 30 per cent profit.

Order forms and invoices

Look at examples to get a full idea of the information you need to include on these, and use your technology to produce them (see page 202-3). Include a repeat order form with every document you sell, and send invoices and hassle letters promptly. Collect regular customers and build up to the cream of selling methods, the subscription list, where neither order forms nor invoices are a problem!

Packing and postage

You will probably begin by storing books at home. Make sure that your stock is covered by insurance. Later, find a local warehouse or ask your printer to rent you storage space. Get a flat table to pack on, plus protective wrapping such as padded bags, sticky tape and stamps that easily make up the amounts required to post your document. Once orders are high, the Post Office can arrange an account, and will collect. Check with the Post Office too for details of their free or cheap start-up mail-outs for new businesses.

Keeping track

From the start, develop a system to keep track of orders, money paid and money owed. From individuals, ask for money up front. If you deal with bookshops, they will expect account terms, and you should send reminders regularly. If at all possible, avoid allowing shops to pay on sale or return.

Keep regular daily, weekly and monthly accounts of money in and out. Take lessons from your accountant, get a bookkeeper to balance your books each month. Also keep detailed lists of your customers and what they buy. This will form an invaluable mailing list when you launch your next document.

Subcontracting

If you can find a distributor who reaches your market, subcontract all the distribution, leaving you free to publicise your document and work on the next. However they do not come cheap; budget for approximately 12 per cent charges and remember that this is on top of any discount shops demand.

Be prepared to wait a while before the profit shows. Our first month's income was £22 and the interest on the bank loan was £53. Hang on in there. We did.

Using the technology to help

One of the most surprising things we discovered when researching this book was the number of people who thought that the usefulness of DTP stopped with the document they were working on. If you are using the new technology to publish your document, then you can also use it to help get that document to its reader. Take the time to find programs for your system which will fulfil the functions outlined here, and you will double your effectiveness as a publisher.

Layout packages

There are many kinds of publishing support material that you can produce on your page makeup package.

If you are at all serious about being business-like, then you will need letterheads, business cards, compliments slips.

If you are selling your product, you will need order forms, invoices, reminders and hassle letters. For marketing, you may want to produce exhibition posters, mail-outs, fliers, a list of the documents you are selling.

Add to this any specialist spin offs if, for example, your publishing centres round a special interest group that needs support material, or a corporate group that needs in-house documentation. Use your facilities whenever you can.

For all these, employ your design skills to the full. Your corporate image will sell your product just as much as the document itself, so even if you can't afford a professional designer for each specific project, get one to develop your house-style for you.

St Mary's *real News*

News
Views
Gigs
Campaigns
Organisations
Diary dates
Agitprop
Essential services
Special features
Local character and
local characters
...everything you
always wanted in a
local paper but always
knew *they* would not

your local independent paper

on sale here

this week...

DTP service here

Your business stationery, leaflets etc prepared to your own design while you wait. Hundreds of styles available.

Word processing

If you can, present every letter you send out to as high a standard as possible; as a personal publisher, people may now be judging you on everything they see you produce. So a good word processing package, used in conjunction with a good printer, may be an invaluable investment. Many word processing packages also have a mail-merge facility which you can use to contact your clients on a regular basis.

Databases

If you have regular contact with your clients, then you will want to set up a client database. This will allow you to manage your clients in several ways. Firstly, you can keep track of clients, their changes of address, their product preferences. Secondly, you can use the data for your mail merges. Thirdly, you will be able to work out what paying patterns your clients have, which are bad payers, which good, and send them reminders accordingly. Lastly, you will use your database to handle your customer accounts. Databases can give you an unbeatable way of keeping in touch with your clients, because they allow you regularly to update your knowledge and experience of large numbers of people.

Spreadsheets

For any kind of commercial publishing, however small the figures involved, you will need accounting facilities. Spreadsheet packages allow you to set up accounts on screen, key in figures which automatically total, and print out regular updates for your accountant. They can also help you calculate the royalties for your authors.

We find particular joy in our financial forecasting package, which automatically tells us how our yearly figures will look with the least little jump in income!

And the rest...

To summarise, we feel that any facility that the new technology can offer you will probably have a place in supporting your personal publishing. Outliner packages could help you brainstorm development ideas, teaching packages could enable you to transfer specialist skills to your entire team, communications packages could allow you to connect your computer to other computers on the other side of the world via the telephone. And computer games can help you enjoy your tea break...

SHELLEY N. NOTT FGA
FREELANCE JOURNALIST

308a Station Road · Harrow · Middlesex · United Kingdom
Telephone: (STD) 01-863 6177 · (INTERNATIONAL) + 44 1 863
Fax: 01-863 9810

SHELLEY N. NOTT FGA

308a Station Road · Harrow · Middlesex · United Kingdom · HA1 2DX
Tel: (STD) 01-863 6177 · (INTERNATIONAL) +44 1 863 6177
Fax: 01-863 9810

CHAPTER

13

WHAT NEXT?

The question 'What next?' is a vital one for personal publishing. Things are shifting very fast, and, whether you are using the new technology or not, you will start to feel the effects of that shift very soon. But exactly what is going to happen?

New technology

DTP itself gets cheaper all the time. In particular, the cost of storing and manipulating the very large amounts of information required for photographic-quality pictures will soon be within the reach of the average personal publisher.

Similarly, printers are falling in cost while improving in resolution. At the moment, laser printers with resolutions over 300 dpi are rare and expensive. The recently invented bubble-jet printers already offer the same resolution, and improve all the time. Since they are also a lot cheaper to manufacture, the average business computer may well be producing typeset-quality (say, 1200 dpi) text and graphics in five years' time.

Once created, however, your document will still need to be reproduced, and here there is no great prospect of change. The offset litho printing machine has as yet no rival when it comes to printing your documents at high-quality but low price – unless it is the bulk photocopier, another seemingly indispensable piece of new technology.

However, in future you may not be so tied to producing batches of documents. Technical reference books, for example, tend to be bought only occasionally but may then be used anywhere in the world. How much easier if they could be transmitted electronically to where they were needed, then reproduced on a laser printer. This system is called *publishing on demand* and is already being used by some universities.

Of course, once you have gone this far, the next question is 'why bother printing it out at all?'. Not only is it possible for a document to be read on screen, but this also carries a number of advantages. Documents can be updated regularly, cross-referencing can be made more efficient and other media such as sound or video can be added. This is called *interactive publishing*, and it is probably here that the real future of publishing lies.

On the following page, we give one example that is a reality now. Although paper publishing is unlikely to be completely replaced for centuries, interactive publishing will probably soon be equally important to you as a consumer and a personal publisher.

Shell Route Finder

If you have ever lost your way whilst driving, you will probably have been faced with a choice. Should you ask directions which may be incorrect, or should you buy a map which may or may be in stock? Here, you have come up against a problem that cannot be solved by conventional publishing. The Shell Route Finder is an electronic alternative that is intended to overcome just this problem.

The Route Finder has been installed on an experimental basis in some Shell service stations to help drivers find their way. It consists of a computer screen that displays a map of the British Isles, set either into the wall or into a console in the centre of the shop.

There is no keyboard or mouse. Instead, the screen is touch-sensitive; simply tapping it has the same effect as clicking a mouse button does. When you tap any given spot on the map, the screen zooms in to give you a more detailed map of that particular area. Tap again, and the screen zooms in again. With four taps, you can zoom in on a map detailed enough for you to see individual streets in any town or village in the country. 'Arrow icons' at the edges of the screen allow you to scroll across a map as necessary.

A 'directions' icon allows you to get full directions from any A to any B in the country. These can appear both on screen and as a printout. The system will even calculate whether you have enough fuel for the journey and, of course, tell you the location of another Shell service station where you might buy more when you need it.

The guts of this seemingly space-age system are an ordinary BBC micro connected to an optical disc drive that contains the maps.

The touch screen is simply fixed over the existing computer's own screen.

The advantages of the system are that it can both hold far more detailed information than could conveniently be published or carried in book form, and that it can give directions and other information. In theory, this could include items that need frequent updating, such as roadworks or special events.

The Shell Route Finder is just one example of public-access electronic publishing. Such systems will be common sights in shops, banks and offices in the very near future.

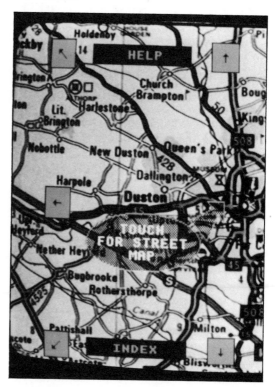

Attitude factor

As we have stressed throughout this book, the personal publishing revolution, though largely caused by the new technology, is not only about that. The effects of the revolution can be seen in attitudes and awareness, even where there is no word processor in sight. We are sure that the publishing *attitude* revolution will continue to spread just as quickly and inexorably as the technology has.

Firstly, expectations of personal publishing will continue to rise, particularly in the corporate field. Whereas five years ago, it would have been perfectly acceptable to present a report neatly typed, in future the expectation will always be for laser output. In an age of four-colour, glossy mail shots that land through our door every day, the document that does not live up to this standard will, in future, be seen as failing.

Secondly, there will be far greater expectations of what support services we have to obtain our finished document. We are beginning to believe that 'even' ordinary people can use the expertise of a designer, the technology of a laser printer. Personal publishers are becoming more aware of the need for professional expertise; and, as expectations rise, so inevitably will the willingness to develop professional skills across the spectrum, and also to ask professionals for support and help.

The professionals too will be more willing to respond. Many times, while researching this book, we came up against professionals who were wary of the personal publisher. However their number and their antagonism was neither as great as we expected nor as great as it was even a year ago.

There are now very real signs of a breakdown in the divisions between personal and professional publishing. Drop-in typesetting bureaux are sweeping the country – happy to deal with those without expensive technology. Instant print shops have swept the country, pleased to deal with those who would die rather than brief a traditional printer. Staff in all these establishments (and in the enlightened traditional typesetters and printers who are fast following suit) are typical of a new brand of professionals who work *with*, rather than *for*, the customer. A cross-fertilisation of amateur and professional is happening apace.

Because of this, we think that the future of personal publishing belongs not to those who are good only with the new technology – although, ultimately, we will all come to be

'computer comfortable'. Rather, it belongs to those who can use the new technology in a personal context, working to channel the people skills and the machine skills together into a whole, new field.

It is not by coincidence that what we have been talking about in this book has been personal publishing – with the emphasis on the word *person*.

What next for you?

Whether you originally picked up this book looking for ideas for a party invitation or guidelines for setting up a corporate magazine, we hope that it has been of use.

In a broader context, we hope it has also helped you see a little more clearly what your real interests are in personal publishing, and what the future holds for you. Where are you going now, in this fast-changing publishing world?

We hope, of course, that the 'what next' will be to go off and do it all over again with a new project. In particular, as we have suggested in Chapter 12, your document may have succeeded sufficiently to let you find yourself, as we did, with a small but fascinating publishing company on your hands. Equally, you may find yourself in demand by others, wanting you to provide a service for them in letterheads, business cards and other DTP products.

Even if neither of these expansions happen, you will have gained a great deal. You will have more knowledge, to inform your appreciation of what really goes into the making of your local paper. You will have more skills, in working with words, images or the new technology. You will have new strategies for dealing with people and with processes. You will have some models of what publishing and the people in it are really like.

Above all, you will know that, even if you never publish again, you are part of an important change in the world today. For the personal publishing revolution has only just begun.

GLOSSARY

Artwork: line illustrations
ASCII: American Standard Code for Information Interchange; a form of computer text understandable by most computers
Bander: a simple, cheap, low-quality pressure method of reproduction
Bézier curves: smooth, flexible curves used on graphics software
Bit-map graphics: graphics made up of dots or bits
Bleed: where the print of text or graphics extends to the edge of a page
Bold: a heavy weight of typeface
Bond paper: a rough, heavy, but high-quality, paper
Bromide: photographic paper used to carry long-lasting versions of text and graphics
Bullet points: small dots used for emphasis or to indicate a list
Byte: a measurement of memory; eight bits, the fundamental units of computer information
Camera-ready copy (CRC): text and graphics presented as a paste-up or otherwise ready to be printed
Cartridge paper: coarse paper often used for envelopes
Character: a text symbol
Clone: a computer system that imitates another system
Column: a vertical block of text
Column-based: page layout software in which the text is fed into the basic unit of a column
Command lines: commands typed into a computer system through the keyboard
Compatibility: the ability to link with another piece of hardware or software
Copyeditor: editor who works to structure text
Copyright: protection from copying for the work of an author or artist
Crop: taking off the edges of an illustration, usually to make it fit
Cursor: a screen pointer that shows your place in the text
Desktop publishing (DTP): publishing using the new technology to produce high-quality output
Die-cutting: a process by which a design is punched out of paper
Document-oriented: a layout where the main unit of work is the document
Dot-matrix printer: a printer that works by impressing pins on to a ribbon
Dpi: stands for dots per square inch, a measure of the resolution of an image
Drop shadow: a shaded area behind an image that adds definition to it

Embossing: a process creating a 3D image on paper by pressing it between two dies

Encapsulation: a process of finishing a page by sealing it in an envelope of plastic

Fat bits: a software facility allowing work with very small-scale sections of a graphic

File: a set of information on computer

Floppy discs: computer discs that store and transfer information

Font: characters of the same typeface

Footer: a section of text that appears on the foot of every page

Footnote: additional text added at the foot of an individual page

Galley: a long strip of phototypeset text used for proofing before page layout

Global: a function such as a search that is repeated throughout an entire file

Greeking: text set as strips of tone or nonsense text to indicate the position of text on a page

Grey scale: a scale of tone from white to black

Grid-based: page layout software based on grids

Gutter: space between columns of text

Half-title: the first page of a document, which comes before the title and is usually blank

Half-tone: processing of artwork containing continuous tone into a form that is easily printable

Hard copy: text on paper rather than on screen

Hard disc drive: a storage unit within or in a separate case from a computer

Hardware: the equipment, rather than the programs, that make up a computer system

Head: a caption or title heading a piece of text

Header: a section of text that appears at the top of every page

Hot stamping: a process that impresses foil on to the surface of paper

House-style: a consistent style of writing developed for a document or series

Hyphenation: adding hyphens to text to ensure more even spacing within a line

Icon: a small screen symbol used to indicate a file or function

Imagesetter: a professional, high-resolution typesetting machine

Imposition: a way of ordering pages before printing so that they will fall in the right sequence in the finished document

Indent: the space left when text is offset relative to the rest of the text in a column

In-house: within the publishing house rather than subcontracted

Ink jet printer: a printer that feeds ink through jets to reproduce images

Inner margin: the margin on the side of the page next to the binding

ISBN: International Standard Book Number

ISSN: International Standard Serial Number

Italic: a type variation that slopes to the right used in serif faces

Justification: spacing text out so that it fits flush with the right and left margin

Kern: moving characters together to give a tighter look

Key in: type into a computer system

Laid paper: a paper with a pattern set into it, often used for notepaper

Lamination: a process of finishing a page by heat-sealing it with a sheet of pvc

Landscape: page arrangement with width greater than depth

Laser printer: a high-resolution printer that uses lasers to reproduce the image

Layout: the way text and graphics are arranged on a page

Leader dots: dots (or equivalent) linking two elements on a page

Leading: the amount of space between lines of text

Letterpress: a traditional pressure method of printing

Line artwork: lines or blocks of colour that do not include shades or tones

Literal: an error in typing or typesetting

Machine varnish: a process of finishing a page by coating it in clear varnish

Margin: the space between the edge of a page and the text

Mark up: written indication on text or paste-up of typesetting or printing instructions

Masthead: the large title of a newssheet

Measure: the width to which a line of text is set

Mechanical: finished work, either paste-up or computer printout, ready to print

Menu: a program feature that lists command possibilities

Modem: a link to communicate between computer systems via telephone lines

Mouse: a hand-sized unit with one or more buttons that rests on the desktop and which is attached to the computer by a flex

Multi-tasking: the ability to run more than one program at once on a computer

Object-oriented: a graphics program that treats a picture as a set of discrete objects

Oblique: a type variation that slopes to the right used in sans serif faces

Offset litho: a standard method of printing

Optical character reader: a machine that allows you to transfer text into a computer.

Orphans: first or last lines of paragraphs or headings left stranded by a page break

Outer margin: the margin next to the outer edge of the page

Outliner: hierarchical, note-making software

Overlay: paper or film laid over pasted-up work to carry extra paste-up or instructions

Page-oriented: a layout where the main unit of work is the page

Pagination: page numbers

Paste-up: to mount text and/or graphics on a backing sheet in preparation for reproduction

Perfect binding: binding a book by gluing pages together and then attaching the cover

Pica: a measurement almost a sixth of an inch

Pixel: a dot, the smallest point you can get on a computer screen

PMT: photo-mechanical transfer, used to create a photographic version of black and white artwork suitable for pasting up

Point: a measurement equalling a twelfth of a pica

Pointer: a screen symbol that points out items on the screen

Point size: a size of typeface

Portrait: page arrangement with depth greater than width

Posterisation: a darkroom technique that makes a photograph look like a poster

PostScript: a page description language that produces high-quality setting

Prelims: the introductory pages of a book

Printers' proofs: a trial print run to allow proofing before a full print run

Print run: the number of documents to be printed at any one time

Proof-reading: checking text for errors

Refresh rate: the flicker rate on a computer screen

Registration marks: marks on paste-up and overlay to allow accurate alignment

Resolution: accuracy and definition of type

Rough: an early version of a drawing/design

Royalty: money paid to an author that is a proportion of the fees earned by her work

Saddle stitching: a method of binding pages by stapling

Scanner: equipment that takes an image and converts it into information that a computer can work with

Screen dump: a picture of the computer screen as seen

Screen printing: a method of printing where ink is pushed through a mesh on to paper

Screening: photographing an image so as to render the tones in the image as a pattern of small dots

Scroll bar: a screen feature allowing movement of the view of a document from side to side and up to down

Serif: a small stroke at the end of any line that makes up a letter

Set solid: type set without extra leading between the lines

Sidebar: a box or bar at the side of a page in which added information is set

Side stitching: a method of binding loose paper by stitching near the margin

Software: computer programs

Solarisation: a darkroom technique capable of creating dramatic special effects

Style sheet: instructions within a computer program outlining style (font, point size, weight, indent etc) for a particular text

Subscript: a facility to allow characters to drop below a normal line

Superscript: a facility to allow characters to rise above a normal line

Synopsis: an outline of a book or article, prepared by an author

Template: a set form into which text or graphics can be slotted

Thermal transfer printer: a printer that uses heat to transfer the ink to the paper

Thermography: a print-finishing process that produces a shiny, 3D effect on paper

Thumbnails: a small version of a page used for planning a document

Title page: the page of a document where the title, and usually the authors' and publishers' names, are included

Tone artwork: illustrations including shading

Trim marks: marks on the final presentation of text to a printer, which indicate where a page is to be trimmed

Typeface: one kind of type, including all the variations of weight, size and style

Ultra-violet varnish: a process of finishing a page with a high-gloss varnish

White space: any parts of a page without text or graphics on them

Widow: a word left alone on a line

WIMP: a computer system that uses Windows, Icons, Menus and Pointers

Window: a program feature that allows viewing of a document

Word processing program: a computer program for writing and editing

Word processor: a computer system whose primary function is writing and editing

Wove paper: a smooth paper often used for letterheads

Wrap-around: a software effect that allows text to come close to an illustration without going over it

WYSIWYG: letters standing for What You See Is What You Get, and describing an easily accessible form of computer system

APPENDIX

Now that this book is *Into Reprint*, we have taken the opportunity to update the appendix for January 1991. In particular, the *Technology update* has been completely rewritten.

Please note that this appendix is for information only, and is not a recommendation. Equally, we take no responsibility for the quality of any of the products or services included.

Books

We have listed here books that add to and give greater detail about topics that we have not had space to cover.

Desktop publishing
The Desktop Publishing Companion, Graham Jones, Sigma Press, 1987
Design for Desktop Publishing, John Miles, John Taylor Book Ventures, distributed by Spa Books, PO Box 47, Stevenage, SG2 8UH, 1987
The Electronic Publisher, Diane Burns, S Venit and Rebecca Hansen, Prentice Hall, 1988 (probably the most comprehensive guide on the market, enabling you to raise your standards to truly professional ones)
Introducing Desktop Publishing, David Hewson, John Taylor Book Ventures, distributed by Spa Books, 1989
Publish!, Nicholas Saunders, available from

Neal's Yard DTP Studio, 14 Neal's Yard, London WC2 9DP (send 80p or 4 first class stamps)

General publishing
Effective Publicity and design, J Zeitlyn, Interchange Books 1987
Graphics Handbook, Richard McCann, The National Extension College, 1986
A Guide to Magazine Production for Churches, Alan Robinson, Kirkfield Publications, 56 Henley Avenue, Dewsbury, West Yorks WF12 0LN (typewritten basic guide for church publishing, containing many helpful hints)
Guide to Self-Publishing, Henry Mulholland, Mulholland-Wirral, The Croft, School Avenue, Little Neston, South Wirral, L64 4BS, 1984 (but with typed update)
How to Publish Yourself, Peter Finch, Allison and Busby, 1987
Marketing for Small Publishers, Keith Smith, (Inter-action Inprint) Interchange Books, 1980
The Print Book, National Extension College, 1986
Print – How You Can Do It Yourself, Jonathan Zeitlyn, Interchange Books, 1986 (another 'get into production' book)
Publishers' Freelance Directory, published annually by Hobson's Publishing (invaluable guide to freelancers)

Miscellaneous

Be Your Own PR Man, Michael Bland, Kogan Page, 1986 (despite the sexist title, a useful guide to getting yourself known)

Creative Handbook, published annually by British Media Publications

Designers' Guide to Colour 5, I. Shibukawa and Y. Takahashi, Angus and Robertson, 1990 (replaces the previous versions 1 to 4)

Dictionary of Modern English Usage, ed. H. W. Fowler, OUP 1983

The Writers' and Artists' Year Book, published annually by A and C Black

The Writers' Handbook, published annually by Macmillan

Exhibitions

Computer Publishing Solutions, held annually; contact Online Ltd, Blenheim House, Ash Hill Drive, Pinner, Middx HA5 2AE, 081-868 4466

Magazines

The Bookseller, 12 Dyott Street, London WC1A 1DF, 071-836 8911 (aimed at professionals, but useful to get a 'feel' for the book trade)

Desktop Publishing Today, Industrial Media Ltd, Blair House, 184-186 High Street, Tonbridge, Kent TN9 1BQ 0732-359990 (subscription DTP magazine but free to those who can show they have responsibility for buying equipment)

In addition, if you have a computer system, you will probably want to buy the support literature. Try:

A&B Computing (Archimedes); *Amiga World* (Amiga); *Macuser* (Macintosh); *Personal Computer World* (mainly PC) and *Byte* (US programmers' magazine very good for helping to predict future trends). Most of these magazines publish occasional buyers' guides which are well worth getting.

Professional associations

The following can often provide lists of members and give advice on rates of pay and contracts.

Association of Illustrators, 1 Colville Place, London W1P 1HN, 071-636 4100

British Institute of Professional Photography, Fox Talbot House, Amwell End, Ware, Hertfordshire SG12 9HN, 0920-464011

British Printing Industries Federation, 11 Bedford Row, London WC1R 4DX, 071-242 6904

National Union of Journalists, 314 Gray's Inn Road, London WC1X 8DP, 071-278 7916

Publishers' Association, 19 Bedford Square, London WC1B 3HJ, 071-580 6321

The Self-Publishing Association, Lloyds Bank Chambers, 18 High Steet, Upton-upon-Severn, Worcs WR8 0HD, 06846-4666 (non-profit making organisation offering practical support to writers who self-publish)

Society of Authors, 84 Drayton Gardens, London SW10 9SB, 071-373 6642

Society of Picture Researchers, BM Box 259, London WC1N 3XX, 071-404 5011

Writers' Guild of Great Britain, 430 Edgware Road, London W2 1EH, 071-723 8074

Standard Book Numbering Agency, 12 Dyott Street, London WC1A 1DF 071-836 8911 (for obtaining standard book/magazine numbering codes for relevant documents)

Technology update

Computer technology advances almost daily. Since this book was written, the following very significant changes have taken place.

Microsoft Windows 3.0 for the PC

Windows is a program that puts a WIMP interface onto a PC (WIMPS are now called a Graphical User Interface or GUI to appease macho programmers). Version 3.0 of Windows is very good and quite cheap (£60). If you buy a PC, we recommend that you also buy Windows 3.0 and only buy programs designed to work with Windows 3.0. In order not to suffer excruciating slowness, however, you must buy a machine with at least an 80386SX processor, 2M of RAM and a hard disc. Our sample system would be:
- Elonex 386SX 2/40 with 14" mono VGA screen, Windows 3.0 and mouse: £985
  Epson EPL7100 laser printer: £800
  PC PageMaker 3.0: £390
  Microsoft Word for Windows: £260
  (because PageMaker 3.0 has no built-in word processor)
  Adobe Type Manager: £70
  Total: £2505

Cheap Apple Macintoshes

A considerably cheaper new version of the Mac Plus (pictured on p108) is the Classic. With 2M of RAM and a 40M hard disc built in, the educational discount price (see p215) is £725. So a complete Macintosh DTP system would now be:
- Macintosh Classic 2/40 with mouse: £725
  BPP PLPII laser printer: £950
  Ready,Set,Go!4.5a: £295
  Adobe Type Manager: £70
  Total: £2040

Another cheap Macintosh, the LC, comes with an equivalent processor to the Elonex PC (see above) and a 14" colour screen, for £1200. This would bring the total system price to £2515.

Outline fonts without PostScript printers

A program called Adobe Type Manager lets you see outline fonts on screen, and, even more importantly, print them without having to buy a PostScript printer. This cuts about £1000 off the price of a printer; the only real drawback is that you won't be able to use PostScript drawing packages such as Freehand to their full potential. ATM is available for both Macs and PCs, and we have included it in our sample systems for those two machines.

An alternative to PostScript called TrueImage, with its own TrueType fonts, will probably appear on both Macs and PCs during 1991. This won't need special printers, either.

New DTP programs

Because of Windows 3.0, several previously Mac-only programs (such as Quark Xpress) are now crossing the divide to the PC. There are also now dozens of low-cost DTP programs, and many word processors now have a lot of DTP features. If you don't need a full-featured package, it is well worth looking through computer magazines for comparative reviews of recent products.

At the top end of the market, just about every package now prints in full colour and sports a list of features as long as your credit limit. Also on the market is Design Studio, a grown-up version of our favourite program, RSG!.

Colour printers and photocopiers

Often one and the same machine, these have now come down in price to the £10-20,000 mark. While they are too expensive for us or probably for you, your local instant print shop may well have one just waiting for your custom.

Other sample systems

These prices were correct in Dec 1990. We publish them to give you an idea of relative costs.

- Atari ST-based system
  Atari Mega 2 ST with monochrome screen: £900
  Atari laser printer: £900
  Calamus layout package: £400
  Total: £2200

- Amstrad PCW-based system
  Amstrad PCW9512 with daisywheel printer: £500
  NewWord word processor package: £100
  Amset direct setting programme: £200
  Total: £800
  (This is our only sample system without a laser printer, so we included Amset to allow you to use a typesetting service.)

Reducing the cost

There are two ways to cut the cost of personal publishing:

Buy Less

- Ask yourself if you really need a colour screen. Monochrome is easier on the eyes, anyway.
- Don't buy that flash graphics program until you are sure you really need it.
- Buy a cheap dot-matrix printer, and take your discs to a bureau for output.
- Don't buy a computer at all! With an electronic typewriter and a tube of glue you can produce a smart, readable and credible newsletter.

Buy more cheaply

- Haggle with dealers; they expect it. Be clear from the start about exactly what you want, or you will not be able to compare like with like.
- Buy from a mail-order 'box shifter'. Of course you won't get dealer support, so set up community support instead.
- Buy through your local school and qualify for an educational discount.

Training

For training in all professional publishing skills, contact Book House Training Centre, 45 East Hill, London, SW18. 081-874 2718. BHTC is the organisation used by most of the big publishing companies.

For training and consultancy in how to set up and manage in-company publishing systems, contact the authors via our company, Transformation Management Ltd, 50 Coleshill Place, Milton Keynes MK13 8DP. 0908-690605.

Desktop Publishing Today magazine usually includes a listing of companies around the country which offer training. See p213.

User groups

Most computer systems have user groups from which you can get day-to-day support as well as a number of benefits such as magazines and conferences.

Amstrad Professional User Club, Enterprise House, PO Box 10, Roper Street, Pallion Industrial Estate, Sunderland SR4 6SN, 091-5108787
Atari Serious User Group, Sigatari, 143 Richmond Road, Leytonstone, London E11 4BT, 081-556 0395
The IBM PC User Group, PO Box 360, Harrow, Middx HA1 4LQ, 081-863 1191
Macintosh User Group, 11 South Parade, Summertown, Oxford OX2 7JL, 0865 58027
PageMaker User Group Membership Services, 572 Wilmslow Rd, Withington, Manchester M20 9DB, 061-448 1141
Ventura User Group, Linda Liddell Associates, Lound House, Forncett St Mary, Norwich, Norfolk NR16 1JP, 050841 580

How this book was produced

This book was written on two MacPluses with Qisk hard discs. The ideas were organised using IdealLiner, and the resource section was gathered using Hypercard. When we came to type the book in, we laid out the pages to a design specification by Anthony Bussey of BBC Enterprises, using Ready,Set,Go! 4.0 and then Ready,Set,Go! 4.5, and finally typed the text straight into each page layout. The pictures on pages 72 and 146 were reproduced using ImageStudio™. ImageStudio is a trademark of Esselte Letraset.

References

The illustration references are as follows.

- Cartoons on pages 7, 8, 10, 13, 18, 24, 26, 40, 42, 48, 74, 75, 98, 101, 105, 106, 163, 172, 190, 191, 194, 195, 201, 206 by Jim Hanson.
- Line drawings on pages 30, 31, 44, 49, 50, 65, 102, 103, 108, 110, 112, 115, 117, 154, 156, 158, 166, 168, 169, 170, 174, 175, 181, 182, 183, 184, 185, 186, 187, 188, 189 by Mike Gilkes.
- Illustrations and screen dumps on the following pages were produced from these programs: 46, 51, 53 (Write Now); 52 (Word Finder); 122, 132 (Aldus PageMaker); 136 (Quark XPress); 142 (Freehand); 144 (MacPaint); 145 (MacDraw); 146, 153 (ImageStudio); 147 (Illustrator); 148 (IdealLiner); 149 (WingZ).
- Ilustrations on the following pages are used courtesy of the people named: 12 Design Effect and RHM, Enigma, Editors and contributors to Holm News, The Last Word; 16 Grapevine Publishing; 27 Hong Kong Restaurant and Prontaprint Barking; 29 Adobe Systems, Stephen Parr and Anne Stevenson, Plain English, Prontaprint Barking and Signs Illuminaire; 39, 78 Design Effect; 41 David Hewson and Mandarin Publishing; 47 Signa Publishing; 52 Diana Bailey; 57 Capital Communications and Typeshare; 59 Design Effect and RHM, Andrew Mortlock, Typeshare; 61 Design Effect, Emma Grimwood and Prontaprint Barking, Jonquil Publishing; 63 Capital Ceramics, Clowns and Prontaprint Barking; 66, 67, Dynamic Graphics; 71, 143 Fingerprint Graphics; 72, 146 Esselte Letraset; 73 John Fuller; 77 Julia Howard; 104, 139 Rank Xerox; 105 Acorn Computers; 118 The

Women's Health and Reproductive Rights Information Centre; 131 Spectrum; 141 Gate Seven Computers; 150, 203 Enigma; 154 Canon UK; 155 Jean Nelson; 157 Signa Publishing; 162 *The Independent* ; 165, 177 Jonquil Publishing; 167 Avon Poetry News; 171 Geoffrey Quarry; 178, 179, 183, The Modern Printers; 180 Wiggins Teape; 184 Point of Sale; 193 Ian Rennie and The Modern Printers; 200 Design Effect and Reid-Adam Communications; 205 Shell UK Oil

Corporate Acknowledgements

These companies have each donated hardware, software or employees' time to this book. We would like to thank them particularly for their contribution.

Acorn Computers
Fulbourn Road, Cherry Hinton, Cambridge CB1 4JN
Aldus UK
39 Palmerston Place, Edinburgh EH12 5AU
Computers Unlimited
2 The Business Centre, Colindeep Lane, Colindale, London NW9 6DU
Esselte Letraset Ltd
St George's House, 195/203 Waterloo Rd, London SE1
Frontline Distribution
Intec 1, Wade Rd, Basingstoke, Hants RG24 0NE
The Modern Printers Ltd
20 Bull Lane, Edmonton, London N18
Rank Xerox UK Ltd
Bridge House, Oxford Rd, Uxbridge, Middx UB8 1HS

Personal Acknowledgements

We should like to thank everyone who has helped us produce this book, particularly:

Diane Bailey of MacUser; Roger Brett of Shell UK Oil; Patrick Brown of Alphabet Set; Sandra Corbin; Peter Cozens of the London Graphics Centre; Michael Crozier and Ciárán Hughes of *The Independent*; Leigh Davies of Agfa Gevaert; Dynamic Graphics; Gordon Fielden of the Society of Authors; Ian Finch of Multum Systems; Fingerprint; John Fuller; Glebe Publications; Dr A T Gower of Spectrum Business Computers; Michael Hardman of Capital Communications; David Hewson; Carlye Honig for her particular contribution to Chapter 8; Julia Howard; Jonquil Publishing; Colin Knight of Midsummer Computing Exchange; Robin Kyd of the Publications Department of the Open University; Barbara Levy; Mr Li of the Hong Kong Restaurant; Michael Lopategui of Design Effect; Surya and Caroline Lovejoy; Mike Meir of Gate Seven Computers; Cheryl Montgomery of Milton Keynes Development Corporation; Andrew Murdoch and Gill Bush of Prontaprint, Barking; Shelley Nott of Engima; Joseph O'Connor of Lambent Books; Stephen Parr; Don Payne of the London College of Printing; Tony Peake of Letraset; Prentice Hall; Lisa Saffron and the workers of the Women's Health and Reproductive Rights Information Centre; Nicholas Saunders and Neal's Yard Desktop Publishing; Signa; Silica Systems; Sintrom; Conrad Taylor; Geoff Thorn at Canon UK; Colin and Frances Wilson of the Modern Printers; Nick Voss-Bark of Typeshare.

Index